30 South/30 North

30 South/30 North

*An experience of living
thirty years in the north and
living thirty years life in the south.*

Leroy Walls

Library of Congress Control Number:		2014908687
ISBN:	Hardcover	978-1-4990-1853-0
	Softcover	978-1-4990-1854-7
	eBook	978-1-4990-1852-3

This book was printed in the United States of America.

Rev. date: 05/08/2014

To order additional copies of this book, contact:
Xlibris LLC
1-888-795-4274
www.Xlibris.com
Orders@Xlibris.com
615516

CONTENTS

In honor of my wife, Novella Walls, my children, grandchildren, great-grandchildren, and the future members of the Walls family.

CHAPTER ONE

Start of My Life

Looking back to the year 1936, I can remember my dad and the rest of my family moving from our hometown in Kentwood, Louisiana. Our new destination was a small town by the name of Fluker, Louisiana. *Fluker, what a strange name for a town*, I remember thinking to myself. That town with the strange-sounding name was going to be our family's new hometown.

Our family consisted of my dad (Willie), my mom (Virginia), my brother (Weldon), my sisters (Velma and Alice), and me. I was the youngest at the tender age of four and probably the most excited. As the truck in which we were all loaded in moved slowly down the dusty dirt road, my eyes tried to cover every inch of scenery through the dust. The sounds were all very familiar, especially the sound coming from the back end of the truck. We had our cow on the back of the truck mooing as if she was asking where she was going. In my four-year-old mind, I recall wondering how we were going to get the cow off the truck. I witnessed the struggle that my dad and mom had trying to get the animal onto the truck. I don't know how long it took for them to load her, but I know I was able to finish breakfast, wash out my dish, repack the bowl, and play four games of marbles before we got that stubborn cow on the truck. I thought about what would happen when we reached our destination, hoping it would be easier for her to get off the truck than what I witnessed getting her on.

The truck continued moving at a slow but determined pace. It seemed to be searching out every inch of the gray gravel road for some type of confidence in what was up ahead. Looking at my mother, I never knew she was under the stress she must have been experiencing at the time. The time was when African Americans were not expected to be regal, strong, and satisfied—but that is exactly how I remember her. She was short in stature but mighty in all other areas of life. She never allowed herself to show any emotions that were far from the emotion of kindness. She was strong, humble, and smart. She was a very unique African American lady taken from this earth at a very young age.

We finally arrived at our new home in the town with the strange-sounding name—Fluker, Louisiana. The house was larger than our previous home, actually a lot bigger. I decided right after seeing the house and investigating the enormous backyard, or what I believed to be the backyard, that I liked the town with the funny name and the new house. The house was old but solid. It needed a new paint job, but other than that, it was a sturdy house. The house was a four-bedroom house, and it had a front porch that made a creaky sound when I walked across it. I can recall going back and forth just to hear the sound the boards made. I could not wait to get our old rocking chair on this porch. The porch's paint was peeling off, and some boards were buckled under, probably from previous owners' children running back and forth over them. The rectangular-shaped porch was one of my favorite places to be when we lived there; it was so inviting. I remember sitting on the rocky and uneven steps listening to Mom and Dad talk about matters of the past. We would sit out there at night looking up into the starry sky, all black except for the stars flickering in and out, while hearing the crickets talk to each other in their own special language. The front porch was where the family gathered sometimes to talk, sing, and pray. Yes, it holds a treasure of memories for me.

As we were unloading the truck, Mom and Dad were wrestling with the cow trying to get it off the truck. The cow was putting up a good fight; it seemed to object to the entire idea of moving. Dad wrapped the rope around his wrist and then around his waist and began to move backward. The cow tilted her head back in an upward motion, at the same time resisting Dad's pulling motion. Mom had, by this time, hopped on the back of the truck with the cow and tried to push the cow forward. I remember thinking about the strength of the cow and wondering why she was resisting so much. I remember thinking how foolish she will feel about resisting our move when she sees all the lush green pasture in our back yard. *She will be so surprised and feel so ashamed. She could eat for days and never put a dent in all the green grass out there.* Just when all these thought were running through my little mind, something happened that changed the dynamics of the picture taking place. In the middle of the struggle, the cow pulled back so furiously that she broke her horn. After that, she gave in and got off the truck.

The house was owned by a family named the Kents. They also owned the ten acres that the house was located on. I later learned that the Kents owned most of the land in the town of Fluker. The house was old, but that didn't matter to me. Mom and Dad had their own room, my sisters had their own room, and my brother and I had our own room. That was not bad for a sharecropper's son.

The Kent family was a large white family in Kentwood. They would hire sharecroppers to work their land for them. A sharecropper would work the land for the owner and, in turn, get some of the profits from the produce after it was sold to the local market. Sharecropping was a big business in the 1930s; it was a way to keep a roof over families' heads. It was an honest profession for African American families. My father and mother both worked the land, and after school, my siblings and I pitched in to help. To be honest, it was more fun than work for me. I recall running through the fields discovering all kinds of the choicest fruits and vegetables. I loved the fresh fruits and berries that you could only find in the wild. The berries were the sweetest, ripping with juices that seemed to be kissed with sugars and molasses rolled up in one. I cannot remember tasting fruit as deliciously ripened as those ripened by the hot Louisiana sun. The fruit seemed to drip with natural sweetness. I wish that everyone could taste the true sweetness and richness of berries. I have yet to experience that taste sensation again.

The town's population was around 150 people. The majority of the people were white except for the sharecroppers who worked the property. There was one general store for everyone. The town had one small café for the locals, and they gathered their faithfully, usually early Saturday morning. The entire town would be there, or at least make an appearance. We lived about five miles outside in the country, so it took us a while to get to the town, but I usually found a way to go to the city at least on the weekend with a sister or brother. When new supplies would come in, we would go in as a family on our wagon and pick up new supplies. The supplies were approved by Mr. Kent, so everyone recognized our family as his sharecroppers.

As sharecroppers' children, we were all expected to work in the fields alongside our parents, and that is exactly what we did. My dad would lead the way by working from sunrise to sunset. I remember watching him work, thinking that there was not a man on earth as determined as he was. He always worked hard, never using his mouth to complain but always offering compliments and encouragement. I loved to hear him call me by his nickname for me. My dad and mom worked so hard, but neither complained much about anything. They made life seem pretty much carefree. Their formula for this calmness in life was love of God and love of family. That is what we lived by and what we were taught, and our family was the better for it.

An example of this way of life was when a cousin came to live with us. He was a man of about twenty-five years of age. I never knew why he came to live with us, but back then, that was not something uncommon. A lot of families helped each other out. No one would ever consider turning a relative out on the street if that relative asked for your help. Our cousin just joined in with the work in the fields and worked as hard as the next person. This relative was from Texas, my dad's place of birth. He was a tall, sturdy man and went by the initials of LC. I never knew what the *L* or *C* stood for, but we children called him Cousin LC.

The house and land was good for farming but bad for modern living. We had to carry water for about a mile and a half because we did not have a well at the house. It amazes me now how children complain about too much work. Imagine if they had to walk almost two miles just to get a drink of water, and then fill buckets of water to bring back home for the family. I smile at the thought. My dad had all the family pitch in to be part of our working household. Our chores consisted of cutting wood for the fire, feeding the chickens, feeding the hogs, and milking or feeding the cows. The girls would do the cooking when we came out of the field, and I would sometimes sit and watch them when they allowed me to.

The good part of working in the field was that you could find watermelons or other fruits that you could eat. The wild-growing fruits were abundant back then, especially out in the open fields. Our vegetable garden was spectacular—my mom and dad made sure of it. We "shopped" out of our garden. We never had to go to the store except for tobacco, sugar, flour, and rice. We got meat from our hogs and chickens, and vegetables from our garden. We also would sell hogs to the local store. This was a big help with our finances. I loved the days that we did go to the store to sell a pig, or hog. I would often go with my brother, and after the sell, I would get treats. I would get one or two pennies that I could buy candy or moon cakes with; a piece of candy only cost one penny, and a moon pie only cost a penny. Remember, this was in the 1930s, and everything was affordable.

At home, among all the great memories, the best memory I have is of the family prayer meeting that we would have every Wednesday night. I remember the family all together in one room where we would sing hymns, read the Bible, and pray. That was the highlight of the week, and sometimes my dad would ask some of the neighbors to come over and join our prayer meetings. This special time was when I began learning about God, the Bible, and Christian living. We had pictures on our shelves that reflected our beliefs. One picture was said to be God the Father; the other, God the son Jesus. Every night, we were expected to say the Lord's prayers, and when we got up in the morning, we were to pray and give thanks to God. That was and still is a ritual that I have practiced throughout my life; it is the most important part of my life. At home during the day, one of us would start a song then the other family member would join in to help with the song. Those special moments in our home made the day go a lot better because of the joyful singing in the house.

On Sundays, we all would get to church. Dad made sure of it. Every Sunday, we would attend church. Dad would load us up in the truck, and off we would go to the little wooden building where all the blacks would gather together to worship and serve God. There would be singing and clapping of hands. There would be shouts of joy and tears of joy. The church has always been a place for blacks to gather and enjoy the service with preaching and teachings. Afterward, we would start the long journey home. Sometimes if there was another service later on in the day, we would visit until the next service started. On some Sundays, it was late into the night when we got home.

My mother worked in the church; she would wear a white dress and sit up front. My father was a practicing preacher, which is why we took serving God so seriously. He and Mom taught us by example—they lived what they preached. My parents were loving and caring people; they would give their last to help someone in need. We were a big family, even for back in the thirties, but we all felt the love that came from my parents. We spread that love among one another for all our lives.

I loved Sundays because when we did get home, we would usually have fried chicken for dinner. Mom would kill a chicken on Saturday to prepare the bird for Sunday's meal. Even when we stayed at church for the entire day, Mom would bring the chicken so we could eat after the first sermon. Some of my best memories are of the wonderful Sundays we would have as a family. I tried so hard to instill those values in my children, especially the most treasured value of worshipping God and my Lord and Savior Jesus Christ in truth and spirit.

I can see my sisters with their braided hair and ribbons flying in the breeze when they would run on the church lawn. I loved seeing the horses tied to a tree or branch so they could not take off and leave their owners stranded. Everyone had wagons they used for transportation down the long dusty roads, but my family owned a truck. We took so much pride in the fact that we were the only black family in our community that owned a truck.

We would pass them on the road on horseback or on their wagons, and some would even walk home. We had the luxury of having a vehicle, but I never remember feeling a sense of being better than any of the other families, and I never witnessed my dad or mom having a sense of superiority. They just felt blessed. The next week would be a repeat as far as church service was concerned.

Mr. Kent owned most of the businesses in the town, so it is safe to say that he felt his help had to be represented, too, in a successful way. I don't know how much he paid his sharecroppers, but I believe it might have been a little higher than the going rate.

I remember, a short time after we moved to Fluker, my mother became very ill with the measles. Before she realized that she had the measles, she was out in the rain working, so the measles developed in an unusual way. The family said that the measles went in her body instead of the normal way of coming out. My mom got very sick, so sick that we had to call the doctor. The doctor, along with my Uncle Handy and a lot of my cousins, came over. The family gathered there day and night praying for a recovery. Mom had been unconscious for about four or five days. My older bother, Weldon, and my sisters, Alice and Velma, were asked to keep the covers on Mom so the covers would not fall off because mom was completely out. My brother and sisters came up with a plan of keeping the covers on Mom by putting two iron rods on each side of the bedcover to hold the covers on Mom. When we were in another room and heard a thump on the floor, we knew that Mom's covers had fallen off. We would run into the room and place the covers back over her. Mom was in this state of unconsciousness for two weeks. We were really worried about our mother. After two weeks, Mom was conscious, and everything was back to normal again.

I was the baby, so I would get special treatment. Dad and Mom would remind my brother and sisters, especially when they went to town, that I was the youngest, and they would get into trouble if I did something wrong. As you can imagine, that made me popular with my siblings, but they never seemed to resent me for that sticky situation. The trip to the town would take half the day, and for a little boy, it would be easy to get in trouble. Mom and Dad kept us pretty busy. We all had chores to do, and they would take the majority of the day if they were done properly. My older sister, Velma, had the job of ironing all the clothes in the house. My other sister, Alice, had to clean the house and make sure the dishes were washed. The boys' jobs were to work outside of the house because all indoor jobs belonged to the female population. My big brother, Johnny Weldon, would feed the hogs, cows, and chickens. He also had to make sure the yard was clean and the pens of the animals were clean. But I was out playing around the yard because I had not been assigned a job, so the job I took for myself was getting my hardworking brothers and sisters in trouble. In a five-year-old's mind, that was a fun way to amuse oneself.

I remember one day while my sister Velma was ironing, I was running through the house and accidentally knocked over the neatly pressed clothes placed on the top of an old cabinet. It was bad enough that I knocked over every piece of clothing that my sister had so neatly ironed, but they all landed in the big stone fireplace that was burning. The fireplace was about five feet wide, and during the winter months, we always had a large fire burning. The clothes started to burn. Panicking, my sisters and brothers tried to salvage as many pieces as they could. This infuriated my sister because, back then, ironing was a whole-day job. There had to be a fire burning to heat the iron to a temperature hot enough to use to straighten out the wrinkles in the clothes. The iron was a big piece of iron wit h a grip for the hand and a smooth bottom in order to place on the fire and smooth over the cloth when it was hot enough. When my parents returned from town and witnessed the scene, they blamed my sister for not watching me closely and allowing me to run through the house.

I remember another time when my parents were gone again, and my sisters were supposed to watch me and make sure that I did not get into trouble. I was watching the hogs, studying their habits. I noticed that the hogs had a lot of straw in their pens. I notice how the hogs' straw was bone dry, and I determined that it was too dry to burn. I went into the house and found a box of matches. Even though I was warned to never play with matches, I turned a deaf ear to the warning. I guess my curiosity got the better of me because I was determined to see if the straw would burn or just smolder. After two attempts to strike the match and failing, the third attempt was the charm. I threw the lit match on the straw, and it immediately started to blaze. The hogs started squealing and hopping around trying to avoid the flames or the heat. My brother jumped in the pen and beat back the fire. Again, when my parents got home, I was not to blame because I was only five years old. My older siblings got in trouble, and I did not get punished at all.

This went on for quite a while until one day when we were in the woods getting wood for the fireplace. I went along with my siblings just to have something to do. Again, they were warned to watch out for the baby and to not let me get hurt. While we were in the woods, I noticed the little squirrels jumping from tree branch to tree branch. What a fascinating sight. I was hypnotized by the squirrels' jumping skills. In my five-year-old mind, I knew that I could jump from limb to limb just like the squirrels. So I climbed up a tree approximately twenty-five- to thirty-feet high. I sidled myself out to a branch looking for a nearby tree to jump to just as the squirrels were doing. There it was, a branch from another tree sticking out about five feet away. In my five-year-old thinking process, I knew I could do it. Well, thinking that I could imitate what the squirrels were doing, I decided to jump to the tree. The last thing I remember was seeing the leaves on the branch. I know that I fell because when I came to, it was late in the afternoon, and I was under a bench on the front porch. To say the least, I was very confused and wondered why I was under the bench. When I staggered into the house, the looks on the faces of my brother and sisters were of disbelief and relief all at the same time. I didn't ever remember seeing them look that way before. I didn't remember ever feeling the way I did at that time. I knew that I grew up that day, and I decided that I was going to work with them rather than against them.

Here is what happened. From my siblings' assessment, I fell to the ground and lost consciousness. They thought I was dead, so they carried me home and pushed me under the bench on the front porch and then went into the house to come up with a plan to tell our parents regarding my demise. That was a wake-up call for me, and I decided to change.

CHAPTER TWO

Moving Again

After living in the house for a year, my family and I moved to another location in Fluker. We moved to another house a half mile from our first house. This house also belonged to the Kents and was just about the same size as the last house with about the same amount of land. The agreement was the same; my dad sharecropped the land and received half of the profits.

There were a lot of good memories at that house, but I do remember a bad experience. I had wet my bed one night, so I got up before dawn and, because I knew I was in trouble, ran away into the field in the backyard. Behind our house, we had an outside toilet, and around the toilet were heaps of straw stacked about five feet high. I remember burying myself in the straw, pulling the straw over myself. I must have fallen asleep because the sound of my sister's voice calling for me woke me up. Through the straw, I could see and feel the early sun's heat. I also could see and hear my sister calling my name over and over. I would not answer because I was sure that I would be punished for wetting the bed. I knew that wetting the bed was a big one as far as "wrong things to do." After 10:00 a.m., the sun was up high, and I could hear my stomach growling from lack of food. I got up and went back to the house, and the family was so glad to see me that I didn't get in any trouble for wetting the bed.

That fall, I started school. The school was a large one-room building with one teacher. The school grades went from first grade through seventh grade. The building was painted white with a red roof. Inside, there were two blackboards, a closet, and approximately fifty wooden desks for students. The teacher was a lady about thirty-five to forty years old. She looked nice enough, but she could get very mean if pushed. She was insistent that the rules be followed. The rules of the school were the common rules that we hear even today. We were to follow the rules set by the teacher and the school. The one hitch back then was that if you did not follow the rules, you would get a paddling. The teachers back then used a wooden plank to spank the students, and they had the parents' approval. Today, if you hit your student, you could possible go to jail. My daughter is a schoolteacher, and she has shared stories with me regarding teachers losing their positions for words they used. Times have changed. Some would argue that paddling should have remained as a disciplinary method in the school system.

After recess, all the students would get in two lines, the boys in one line and the girls in the other. The teacher stood at the door and would ring a bell that meant recess was over. As the teacher stood at the door, I would imagine that she was counting the students as they came in. The line was a long one with the younger students in front and the older ones at the back. After we marched into the building, we all had separate seats on a long wooden table. We were not allowed to talk while we were in class, and if one student broke the rule, the teacher would strap or paddle them. That was how it all worked. Each rule had a certain number of "licks" if broken. For instance, if you broke the rule by talking, the punishment carried a paddling of five hits/swats. If you broke the rule by chewing gum, you would get two swats. All punishment rules had their own penalties.

The school had an outside toilet similar to the one we had at home. I was always afraid to go to the toilet because I thought that if the bell rang, I would not hear it, and I didn't want to suffer the consequence. I remember coming into class one time wanting to use the bathroom but too afraid to ask the teacher if I could be excused to go to the toilet. I sat there in misery until my bladder could no longer hold out, so I wet my seat. The teacher had my older sister take care of me. She fussed while cleaning me up and threatened to tell Mom if I did not get my act together. That was another growing-up moment for me. I decided that I would use the outside toilet at recess—no matter what.

Part of the reason I did not go to the bathroom at recess was because I liked to play the different games we used to play on the school grounds. I did not want to miss one moment of the excitement. When I started school, I was a bit shy and reluctant to play with the other students. The only ones I felt comfortable with were my siblings, but they had their own friends to be with during recess, so I just sat back and watched. That was my attitude until the growing-up moment of my wetting my seat. I decided that I would come out of my shell and meet people and join the activities. So at recess time, I discovered that I really enjoyed playing games and laughing and talking with other children. That was the start of my understanding that I had a great personality and that people did want to be around me without being forced. The best game in the world for me was baseball. I was chosen to be first base because I was good at catching. I was always chosen first in my group to be part of the team because I was good at catching, but I was even better at hitting. For me, baseball was a way to have fun but keep active at the same time. I came out of my shell and just started having fun.

Another game that we played at recess was called war. I didn't like this game because it was dangerous and was not supervised at all. The teacher took her break inside and never really knew what was going on outside. She came out at the end of recess ringing her bell for us to come back to class. War was the type of game that would be barred from playgrounds today and should not have been allowed back then. The game was a tragedy waiting to happen. In the game, we would choose ten players for each team. The players would split in two lines and spread approximately forty feet apart; the students would be facing each other. The students would be given two or three minutes to find their ammunition for war. The students would be given a command and then start throwing their collected objects at each other. The objects were usually rocks, cans, sticks, and other dangerous objects. I guess we were taking the word *war* literally.

I went along with it because, at that time, I had built a reputation of being athletic and tough. So I went along with the idea, but inwardly, I hated it. We played the game until a tragedy occurred. I'm so thankful to God that it wasn't me who got hurt. While playing the game, a boy got hurt. One kid threw a bone with sharp edges, and it hit the boy in the eye. The boy fell to the ground in agony, holding his hand over his eye. Blood started to seep through his fingers while holding his hand over his eye and head. By this time, the boy started to roll from right to left, screaming. All of us were in shock, I'm sure, so it took a second or two for us to respond. I took off running for the teacher who was inside the school. She came over and tried to help, but he started screaming even louder.

That experience was an eye-opener for me; it taught me that if something isn't appropriate, I should say so. The incident also caused us to get a stern reprimand from our teacher. I discovered that words can hurt more than a paddling. She talked with us about safety, and how something inside of us should warn us about right and wrong. She then asked us a question that I will never forget, "How would you like to be called one-eye for the rest of your life?" I remember thinking how horrible that would be to only have one eye, especially since I loved running through the woods and climbing trees. She then looked at us and said sternly that he would lose the use of his eye forever. So we never played the game again.

School was fun, but after school, we had the usual fights. My younger sister, Alice, got in a fight one time, and she stabbed the girl in the hand with her pencil. She had just sharpened her pencil, and I have always wondered if she sharpened it for the fight. My sister Alice was a fighter— she did not take too much from anybody. She stood up for herself all the time. My older sister was a lot calmer; I guess that came from being older and more mature. She was left in charge of the house many times and was given the authority of a parent. Both of my sisters were good sisters, and I love them so much.

After school, we had five miles to walk before getting home, so we were all delighted to get home and find potatoes boiling on the stove for our after-school snack. We were allowed to get a couple and then begin our regular chores. We did it all: chop the wood, feed the hogs, feed the chicken, and carry the water from the well to the house for the evening. After that was done, we usually headed out to the field to help our parents.

Family was a big part of life back then. Today, we don't value family as we should. Back then, it was unheard of to not help out a family member, but now it is definitely not the case. I remember my aunt Hon and her husband visiting. They along with their two children, Alice and Henry Lee, came for a visit. I loved when they would come to visit because Mother would be in such a good mood. She loved having them there, and so did Dad. They all would sit on the porch and talk for hours. Mother would be so happy, and Dad would be so full of energy. Sometimes I would hear them discuss hunting, fishing, and just life in general. It was a good time for us all. We loved playing with Alice and Henry. They were kids like us—they loved being outside. We would go to the woods and find assorted fruits and berries to eat, or we would let our imagination run wild. But the most fun we'd have was when we would make rocking horses out of trees. The smaller trees, we would bend over and straddle them. As the tree tried to go back straight, we would use our weight to force it back down. This would happen repeatedly; it was a nice makeshift rocking horse. Sometimes we would just find a long stick on the ground and straddle it and pretend it was a real horse. We would run around the woods shouting "go horse!" while we hit the stick with our free hand demanding it to go faster. Our cousins were right there with us having just as much fun as we were. We enjoyed them so much. They liked to play hide-go-seek. As one of us would count, the rest of us would go and hide in the woods. Imagine all the wonderful hiding places that there were in the woods. When it was time for our cousins to leave, we hated it because we knew it would be a while before we would see them again. Aunt Hon lived in a small town called Independence, Louisiana, about twenty miles from Kenner.

Growing up as a black child in the South, we had to improvise a lot when it came to keeping ourselves occupied in the area of fun. I liked to be in the woods. I loved finding the food trees—trees such as apple, pecan, blackberry, and any other trees that supplied edible delicacies. But not every tree was good for food, and it took wisdom to discern what tree you could eat from and what tree was not safe. What I would do was look at the animals—a squirrel, for example. If the squirrel did not eat the fruit, then I would not eat it. The same went for the bird. If I witnessed a bird eating something I was not familiar with, then I would try it; but if I saw a bird shun a fruit or vegetable I did not recognize, then I would follow the bird's advice. You learn certain codes as a young child in the South. The one animal that no one observed when it came to eating was the pig. The pig would eat anything, even poison, and live through it. But of course, a human would die if he ate or drank poison.

I learned a lot from the animals growing up in the rural South back in the thirties and forties. A dog knows what kind of grass to eat if he gets sick. A squirrel, cow, and rabbit all know what grass to eat if they get sick too. I learned from the bird as well. Dad made a birdhouse in front of our house. It was on top of a pole about twenty feet high. The B—. would come by every year to make a nest. All spring and summer, we would sit on our front porch and watch the birds fix their nest and prepare for their newly arrived baby birds. The B— was a very important bird to the farmers because they would keep the hawks away from the farmers' chickens. I learned a lot from the animals, and I passed this knowledge on to my family when I became an adult. We had dogs that we used for hunting rabbits or squirrels. We would wait until it was dark outside to hunt for possum or coon. We would make it a family event. My uncle Ted was the oldest man in the group. He was in his late fifties or early sixties (I don't know his exact age, but that is the age group I would put him in). In my opinion, this uncle of mine was so smart he could look up at the sky on a clear night and find the seven stars that were shaped like a dipper. He then would tell the rest of us to follow him. We really never had to worry about getting lost no matter how far out we wandered because he would look up and find the big dipper to direct him either north or south. I wondered if he could read or write. It is amazing how nature was used in so many instances back then to lead and direct people. I learned a lot in school, but I learned more outside of the little one-room building we called school. These hunting trips usually happened on Friday nights, and I was glad because I did not have to go to school the next day. I could sleep in late on Saturday. We would be out really late, sometimes until early morning. It was nice to know you could walk on any road at night and not be afraid of anyone doing you any harm.

CHAPTER THREE

Harvest Time

At the end of each year, my dad would harvest the crops and check with the owner to see what his bill would be, and then we would move on to the next sharecropper's station. The next house we moved into was also owned by Mr. Kent. Again, we had around ten acres of land to work. By this time, I was old enough to understand the process of sharecropping and farming. I understood that this was a job as well as a way of life—a life that I wasn't sure if I liked or not. I do know that I really enjoyed the adventures that moving once a year carried with it. I especially respected my parents for finding a way to provide for us to make sure we did not want for anything. This new house was different from the other house we sharecropped. This house had a dairy barn about one-half mile in front of the house. This meant we could get dairy products such as milk, butter, and cream. It also meant we could catch a ride to the store with the milk truck. My older brother would work part-time there for a little extra money. He could earn twenty-five cents or even fifty-cents—that was good money in 1938. Adults would get only fifty cents a day on most jobs. At this new house, a number of incidents happened that I would always remember. I, until then, thought that I understood change and what it meant to have change occur on a continuous path, but I discovered that I did not understand change to its inner core. It didn't matter that I was a sharecropper's son and had to move practically after each harvest. The changes that happened at this house, at that stage in my life, left me with a lasting impression. I still remember all the life-altering changes I experienced after we moved in to this house.

After we moved in to the house, Mom and Dad would leave us alone more often than usual because they both went to work outside of sharecropping. They were trying to make that fifty-cents-a-day pay. My sister was in charge of getting us the food we needed for lunch and dinner. My older brother, who was seventeen, and I, being seven, depended on her getting our lunch. She would prepare for us milk and bread. My older sister, Velma, was always looking after me. She would clean up after me when I finished eating. One day, she accidentally washed our bowls out with kerosene oil thinking it was water. The oil is clear like water, so she just assumed it was water—but when she put the milk and bread in the bowl, it was clear that it was not water. Our entire meal was ruined. We went without a meal that day until Mom and Dad came home from work.

We loved milk and corn bread, and we I still enjoy a good bowl full. Mom would bake a big pan of corn bread. The bread would rise so golden brown, and the corner of the bread would be crispier than the rest of the bread and would last longer in the milk. The corner was a desired piece of the corn bread. My oldest brother would sometime cut all four corners and put them in his bowl. I, being the youngest, would just look at him in disbelief, but I never said a word. The same with my sister Velma, she would not say a word either. But my sister Alice would not be silent.

"I want a corner, Weldon," she would say.

He would ignore her or argue with her until the two of them started fighting. My brother would hit and then run around the house with Alice chasing him vehemently. She would always have something in her hand to hit him with. I remember one time, he was running from her and she was on his tail, but he was getting farther away. He turned the corner of the house and looked back to see where Alice was, and she threw a piece of leather from an old horse saddle and hit JW over the eye. Immediately, a knot came over his eye about two inches long. JW began to yell and run holding his head and eye. He was screaming, "My eye! She's crazy!" and I believe he was crying. When Mom and Dad got home, to my surprise, my brother and sister acted as if nothing happened. I don't know how he explained away that knot on his head, but they made it seem like everything was under control. I discovered then that not everything had to be spoken of. In the past, I would have told Mom and Dad what happened, but I knew that I was to say nothing of the incident to my parents. No one told me not to tell; I just knew that it was best left alone.

Another event that sticks with me happened at this house—it was what happened one Christmas Eve. Every Christmas, we would have a man to dress up like Santa Claus. So in 1937, we were all at home, and it was approximately 10:00 p.m., but we were not yet in bed. The house had a window by the fireplace with a shelf on the outside of the window for flowers. Beneath that shelf, there was a wood stack we used to stack firewood. While we were in the living room, someone in a Santa Claus suit came to the window, and we could tell he was standing on the wood stacked underneath the window. When I looked up, I saw the man in the Santa Claus suit getting ready to come in through the window. My dad started yelling, "It's too early! Go back!" But the man kept trying to come in through the window. So Dad got his twelve-gauge shotgun and fired it two times, and whoever it was jumped off the firewood stack and started running. It seemed as if I heard some reindeer running, but I'm sure now it must have been the horse hooves as he was making his escape. I thought that was the real Santa Claus, and I knew we were not going to get our presents because my dad had shot at Santa Claus. I was sad the entire night. Our usual Christmas gifts were two oranges, two apples, candy, and some pecans. We would set our boxes out under the tree and eagerly get up the following morning delighted to receive those precious gifts over again. It seemed that those oranges and apples tasted differently from the ones we would eat throughout the rest of the year. We would also go outside to the road to see if Santa Claus dropped anything off his sleigh. We sometimes would find candy along the road that we gleefully picked and devoured. It amazes me that Mom and Dad were so much ahead of their time when it came to child-rearing. I now know that they would sprinkle candy on the side of the road for us to find, keeping the allusion of Santa Claus and all the great wonders alive in our hearts and minds. We were a happy bunch of children even if some might not understand what our joy was all about. We thought that Santa lost this candy as he was making his home deliveries.

We were now living near my uncle Handy's—that's where we would get our well water. The water was so cool and tasty, and it seemed to have a sweet taste to it as it floated down my throat. The well had a bucket about six inches wide and three feet deep. We lowered the bucket into the well with a rope and pulled the bucket out the same way. The well itself was covered with a wide plank so the birds, rats, and other critters could not scurry into the well water.

The well wasn't the biggest attraction at this house. The yard was covered with all sorts of trees and lots of space to play different games. We would still climb trees and ride the small trees down, pretending that they were horses to ride. We would collect all the straw we could find and pile it all together so we could jump in the piles and then cover one another with the straw. We would go crab-fishing in the creek by our house. We would make the poles from sticks we found, and the bait would be meat scrap. After catching the crayfish, we would take them home to Mom for her to fix. She had a number of different ways to fix the now sought-after delicacies. Mom would boil and eat the tail and use the rest for her delicious gumbo. How I loved those days when we cooked gumbo! The entire house would be filled with the delicious aroma, travelers passing by would comment on how good our dish smelled.

The weekend was nice, but on Monday, we were back to school again. We would have the long five miles to walk to school. The owner of the land that we sharecropped was on two to four hundred acres. He used some of the land for raising cattle; the cattle would run free to graze over the lush pastureland. He owned over five hundred cattle, and he also had buffalo. On our way to school, it would be quicker to cut across the land rather than walking around the property. I remember one day when we were taking our usual path to school, my sister Alice was wearing a red cap. We did not realize that this would excite the bull until we acknowledged that it was charging toward us, running as fast as he could. We ran for cover, all four of us. My brother, JW, ran and jumped across a creek that was five or six feet away, so we all followed him, one after the other, jumping across this creek. I was the youngest, and when it was my turn, I jumped right in the middle of the water. My clothes and everything became soaking wet. I did not have time to worry or cry over my dilemma because the bull was still coming. I managed to get out of the creek just in time to crawl under a fence and into a field for safety. We decided to stay put until the menacing bull had left. After he left, we continued our five-mile journey to school. I was nearly dry by the time we arrived at school.

We would always try to get to school on time because in those days, the teacher was allowed to give you several licks for being late. After school ended, it was the same route home. I learned a lot in school, but I learned a lot by just living. The bull incident taught me how to survive. It was man against beast. I won because I always made it to school. Sometimes I wonder what would have happened if the bull had caught any of us. Would he have amused himself by tossing us into the air and letting us land on the ground, a stunt that I've seen them do so often on television, or would he have gorged one of us to death? I am so thankful to God that I will never know the answer to that question.

CHAPTER FOUR

School Days

I n school one day, an envelope was on the teacher's desk from a place labeled Coca-Cola Company. The teacher opened the letter, and there was a sheet of paper with very few words on it. The paper read "Rule #1. Do unto others as you would have others do unto you." That paper and those words had such a powerful effect on my life. I follow those rules today and have passed them along to my children and grandchildren.

That same year, I learned that my dad had more children before he married my mother. I knew he had two children, a girl and a boy, that lived in Texas. My dad would often visit them in Houston, Texas, even with Texas being over three hundred miles from Fluker, Louisiana. He would make this journey by catching a freight train and "hobo" there and back. *Hobo* is the term used to describe the large number of men, and sometimes women, who would get on one of the empty cars and ride the freight train from one end of the country to the next. These guys would hop off if they see a destination that interested them or until they recognized their intended destination. Either way, this mode of travel back then was common; a lot of men used the freight train instead of the usual passenger train. Sometimes my dad would have little or no money, but he would go and come back successfully. Although he chose this way of travel when he went far off, my dad did have a car. He had what was called a Model A.

I remember Dad and his Model A; I would love to see him pull up in the yard driving his car. I especially liked to see the car at night because of the large bright-white headlights. I recall one night as I spotted those two lights in the dark background (which always reminded me of two moons in the night sky), I ran toward the car to open the gate so Dad could pull the car into the yard. As I was running toward the lights, I fell, tripping over a large piece of wood. I yelled out in pain—a great deal of it was coming from my leg. I am thankful for streetlights now. Back then, there were no lights to help us see what was on the road or ground at night.

We occasionally did drive the car out of town for trips. I loved those times because I knew we were going someplace special—someplace where there would be family, love, and happiness. On one of our few trips in the car, we were driving to Houston, Texas, to visit relatives. When we arrived at Baton Rouge, we had to cross on a boat. The dock was set up on a hill-like surface. Dad came down the hill so fast that I thought we were going to run straight into the river. I wasn't afraid because in my seven-year-old mind, I thought the car would just float across the river. We arrived in Texas at the house of his sister, Aunt Pauline.

My aunt, everyone called her Pal, had her own business. She was a beautician, and she made a handsome salary. She lived in a beautiful big home by anyone's standard. She had a line of customers, both men and women, always wanting their hair fixed, and my aunt would be ready to make them all look pretty. My dad also had two brothers, two sisters, and a son and daughter by his first wife. I had the opportunity to meet all of them for the first time on that trip.

On this trip, Mom only took me. The others stayed at home with our cousin Smoker and his wife. I guess Mom didn't want to leave me at home because she knew I would get the older kids in trouble. The trip took about two days; three hundred miles is a lot to cover. I saw a lot of things on the trip. The cities we went through were fascinating to me. Dad would often stop the car, and we would all get out and walk around to stretch our legs, use the bathroom, and anything else that needed to be done.

The one memory that sticks out from that visit was meeting my dad's son by his first wife. He was twelve and I was seven, so we had so much fun playing together. We would ride bikes, play games, investigate nearby streets, and we would go to the store for Aunt Pal. He showed me sights in the big city that I never would see in a small town like Fluker. The city itself had a population of one hundred thousand people. I was used to Fluker with its population of two hundred people, and everything was new and different. My stepbrother's name was Cleavon, but everyone called him Po-bo.

After I had been there for a week and had been to the store with Po-bo plenty of times running errands for Aunt Pal, I felt somewhat comfortable with my surroundings. So one morning, after learning Po-bo had gone to the store to run another errand for family, I decided to go to the store too. I imagined I would meet him at the store and that we would walk home together. I had been to the store before and knew how to get there, so I really did not think it would be a problem. So off I went to find Po-bo at the store. When I started to cross the six-lane highway and cars were coming so fast, I stopped in the middle of the highway. A lady passing by in her car yelled out of her car window at me, "Boy, you better get out of the way before you get run over!" I managed to get across the traffic to the other side and continue my journey to the store. I made it to the store but never found Po-bo. He had gone to another store. In my small town, there was only one store; it never occurred to me that Po-bo may have gone to another store. The concept was not yet part of my thinking process.

When I got back, I was scolded about my antics and told never to do that again. My mother was so worried about me. I never did that again. I was often reminded that when Po-bo or anyone would go the store, it did not mean they were going to the same store because there were over two hundred stores in that area alone. I decided to enjoy the familiar things that this vacation offered. We children would play a game called china ball in the tree located in my aunt's backyard. It was fun to climb the tree; it reminded me of climbing trees in my small town of Fluker. This made me feel older. I was only seven, but I felt like a teenager living in Texas for that two-week vacation. This was a large part of my growing up because when I got home, I could tell my siblings about my trip. I had been to another state. I had been outside of the small town of Fluker. I could tell my friends about the big city life. I could also show them through my stepbrother's eyes because he came back with us.

This addition to our family made the family larger. Now there were three boys and two girls. We had a large house and there was never a dull moment. Po-bo and my oldest brother, JW, were around the same age, and they did not get along. They had maybe a two- or three-year difference in their ages. Home life was different because as soon as Mom and Dad left, they would fight. I remember one fight when one of them grabbed the gun that Dad kept in the house. The gun was fired, and a hole was created in the top of the front of the house. I didn't understand why JW did not get along with Po-bo. We had cousins over all the time, and he did not fight with them the way he always fought with Po-bo. This made me sad because I loved both of them.

Po-bo was never happy at our house; he often begged to go back to Texas. Dad would not listen. We had too much farm work to be done such as picking cotton and pulling corn. Po-bo made the adjustments, and I tried my darnedest to make him feel welcomed. I remember reminding him of the house we saw in Texas that was made of old car-license plates. It was so unusual—a house made from over two thousand car-license plates. We would often laugh about how I tried to get to the store by myself, and we reminisced on other things about Texas. I think it helped because he seemed to settle down and the fights decreased, but Po-bo still complained about wanting to go back to Texas. He did not like farm work.

At the end of the year, we moved again. We moved to a house that our uncle had lived in when he sharecropped. Uncle Handy and his family moved to a place called Pine Hill, Louisiana. My uncle had saved up enough money to buy his own place. I had mixed feelings about them moving. I would miss my cousins (his children) as we had a lot of fun playing together. My mother and Uncle Handy had children that were close to being the same age. We always played together and saw each other daily. Now all that would change. I never worried about being bullied at school because, back then, cousins fought together. Uncle Handy and my grandmother were sister and brother, so this made Uncle Handy my second cousin, and his children my third cousins. All we knew back then was that we were family, and no one messed with family. I would miss my uncle and cousins, but I enjoyed not having to carry water anymore. Uncle Handy's old house was where the well was located, so now that we moved in his old house, that meant no more struggling with transporting water back to our house. I could just walk out the front door and go to our well. This would be the first time since we arrived in Fluker that we would have our own well in our yard. I was happy about that. We were on the same man's land and still sharecropping.

CHAPTER FIVE

Family Changes

T his was the first time that I really understood change. The family seemed to change; some changes were good and some were not so good. I was eight years old at the time, and I was trying to be a big boy. The family had increased, and we had moved to another location. This location had new owners, the brother of the man who we had been sharecropping for throughout our stay in Fluker. The new house was about a mile from the old house. One day while my dad was burning trash outside in the woods, the fire looked a lot larger than usual. We were playing the usual games we played when we were outside doing outside chores. Dad always insisted that he take care of the fire because it was one of the most dangerous jobs on the farm.

This particular day, I found out just how dangerous the task of working with fire really was. The flames started out small, a bright mixture of orange and blue light rising above the brown sticks and extra brown paper bags used to start the fire. I was consumed with play until I heard my father's voice with that serious overtone. My dad was not a man who angered easily; he seldom showed emotions of fear or anger. So when he changed his demeanor to an extreme, we all knew something serious was happening.

I remember seeing the flames at about five feet high; I had seen them that high before but not at the onset of the fire. The flames always started off low and then gradually rose, but this fire was different. The flames were shooting out in all directions. My dad grabbed a huge bush to try and contain the fire, which took on a mind of its own. Dad yelled for the children to get back. The other adults grabbed anything they could find to battle the flames. Being that we were out in the woods, it would have been useless to run the mile or so to retrieve water from the well. My dad tried everything he could to keep the flames from not reaching anything valuable, but it was to no avail. The flames attacked a nearby old house located on the property and burned it to the ground. That was my first time seeing a house burn, and I did not like the scene at all. My stomach felt queasy, and I felt light on my feet. The house was all blackened and charred. It looked like a pile of coal that was on its way to becoming an extraordinary structure. Dad thought the owner would be very upset and make him pay for the old, dilapidated building. I heard my dad say that "the owner is going to shit a flapjack with a strain of syrup behind it." He meant that the man would be very upset. But to Dad's surprise, the man was not upset at all. He didn't care about the house because it was so old. The house had not had a tenant in years; it was a very old, old house.

So we continue to farm the land and completed the year living in that same area. It was beautiful land with lots of good farmland. The trees were tall and green with lush grass growing as far as the eyes could see. It was a good place to fish and hunt. The creeks were filled with teams of bluegills in it that could be seen through the clear, sparkling water. There were all sorts of life in the creeks and rivers on the property. I liked the hunting best of all. There were rabbits and squirrels to hunt. My brother JW would use his rifle to hunt. I was too young to use a gun, so I used my slingshot. I would take a rubber band and a piece of leather to hold the rock in place. If made correctly, you could shoot the rock about fifty feet to kill your prey. I had a lot of fun with the slingshot gun; the best part was making it.

We moved back to the old house, but we continued to farm the land that was a mile away. We had lots of relatives close by, and I truly loved and enjoyed their company. I remember my aunt Lilly, a very sweet lady. She always had kind words and always had a bright smile on her face. I recall having to go to her house for well water. Our well had dried up, and we had to find other water sources. Aunt Lilly had a well, and she would allow us to get water from it. My sister and I were on one of these missions one evening. When we got about a block from her house, I could smell the fragrance of freshly baked buttermilk biscuits. My mouth started to water, saliva formed, and I swallowed hard. I hoped that this magnificent smell was coming from my aunt's house. I remember looking at my sister, and by the expression on her face, I knew she felt the same. The aroma was hypnotic; I love the smell of bread baking even to this day. When we arrived at Aunt Lilly's house, she was in her usual good mood, always smiling, always kind—and always baking. I complimented her on how good the biscuits smelled and asked if I could have one. Of course she said yes, and my sister and I sat at the table together and enjoyed the biscuits and milk. After we finished, we got our water and returned home. To my surprise, my sister told my mom that I went to Aunt Lilly begging for food. My mom lectured me about how rude it was to beg for food, even from relatives. After the lecture, she gave me a good spanking to remember our conversation. So I learned from that experience, and I never again would ask Aunt Lilly for a biscuit if my sister was with me.

I began to wise up. Being eight years old, I felt as though I needed to do things on my own. When the family was working in the fields, it was my job to bring water, coffee, food, or whatever they might need from the house. The journey was about a mile and a half, but that was not a long journey back then. I had to cross over creeks and wade through grass taller than I was to get to my family in the fields. I really did not mind this job; I felt this was one of the most important jobs in the world. I felt this way because when I showed up, everyone was happy to see me. They would say things like "okay, good ya here," and that me made feel good on the inside. It made the journey worth every moment, even avoiding the poisonous snakes. There were all sorts of snakes in the tall grass that I had to go through, and I remember running from a number of them. I did not let that deter me because, even at that young age, I knew how important family was, and I would never allow them to be disappointed by my actions. Family was important to me and still is very important to me. Back then, there was one person in our family who was very important to me. He was my little brother. My mother had another baby, and we were all very happy about his arrival. I would wash his clothes and rock him in his bed until he fell asleep. The baby made me a big brother, and I took my role seriously. I was always close by in case he needed anything. My joy turned to sadness because after a couple of weeks, my brother died. I was so sad and did not understand what happened at all. My mother explained to me that God wanted him back in heaven, and he had to go home. She told me that he was happy in heaven. I felt happy again because I knew I would be going to heaven when I die and that I would see him again. It would be a family reunion with all of us in heaven with God and Jesus. I went about the day as thought it was a regular day, and time seemed to pass fast because we were happy.

CHAPTER SIX

On the Farm

Some days on the farm were so cold. In Louisiana, when it hit the thirties, it was cold. Very cold. The animals that we normally hunted were scarce, only coming out to look for food. We would occasionally see birds in the yard searching for a crumb to consume or take back to their nest. My dad would sometimes make a trap for them; he would get a long board, about six feet long, and place a string on the board about three feet long. He would tie the string on the board and hold the other end in his hand. Peering from the window, if he saw a bird under the board, he would pull the string, and the board would fall on the bird, trapping it under the board. That would be our supper on some days. This would happen in the mornings, but most of the time, the temperature would rise after noon when the sun would come out. My brother would go out and hunt if the temperatures would rise enough to bring out the rabbits or squirrels. He would sometimes bring home two or three rabbits at a time for food. Mom would cook the rabbits or squirrels, and we would have a nice dinner. My favorite parts were the legs and backs. For me, that part of the rabbit tasted the best.

At night, we would also go hunting. There were about eight men and as many children. I remember, when we were out in the woods, we would build a fire and cook potatoes we brought from home. Our dogs were the real hunters when we hunted at night. They were trained to hunt for rabbits, coons, possums, and squirrels. We would let them go through the woods and find game, while we sat around the fire and cook the potatoes and talked. Whenever we heard them barking loudly and consistently, we knew that they had found something, and we would run to their location. Sometimes we stayed by the fire, and sometimes we went with the dogs. I loved going out in the woods at night because it made me feel like a big boy. We would stay in the woods for hours; this was how the younger kids were taught how to find food on their own.

I was taught a lot of survival skills as a young boy—that was the way of the South. Another skill I was taught was how to get back home after a long night in the woods. We would go deep into the dark woods about five to six miles away from home. Upon returning from the woods, still dark at night, we would sometimes get lost. My uncle Ned taught us boys how to look into the night sky searching for certain stars. There were many stars in the night sky along with the moon. Uncle Ned pointed out the stars shaped like a dipper and taught us how to use those stars to get back home. It was amazing to me that my uncle used the same group of stars that the slaves used to escape slavery. We would just follow Uncle Ned, and after two or three hours, we would be back home safe and sound.

Those hunting trips were taken on the weekends because we could not go hunting at night during the week. On weekdays, because of school, we had to go to bed at 8:00 p.m. so we could get up at 5:00 a.m. to do our work before getting ready for school. We all had a job to do before going to school; my job was getting the wood for the fireplace or stove. I had to stack it by the window after carrying it from the woods. Every day in the South, that was the familiar routine for the boys and some girls. After doing our chores, we had to meet the teacher's deadline to arrive at school on time. If we were late, we would get twelve licks on our hands from the teacher. The teachers did not accept excuses, and that was the way it was back in the mid-1900s. On the way home from school, the trip was always interesting because there was usually a family fight. Back then, the cousins would fight together, and of course, the brothers and sisters helped each other out. I guess it is safe to say that there was never a dull moment on the farm.

At the end of each school year, there would be a school program. It was something that the schools put on as an end-of-the-year treat. All the students would have a poem to recite, or a group of students would perform a skit of some sort. The teacher always gave my sister and me a long poem to recite. It was often more than three pages long. I could not read that well, so my sister would read my lines to me, and I would memorize them word for word. I also memorized my sister's part just for the fun of being able to tell her what she would say next. I enjoyed the end-of-the-year programs; they got everyone involved. All the parents and students would laugh and have such a good time. It was the perfect atmosphere to usher a beautiful summer in to full bloom. I can even remember the words sung at the end of the play. It went like this:

Our little meeting is about to break, and you and I must part.

May God Almighty bless you if I never ever see your face again.

I love you to my heart.

Farewell, my schoolmate.

May God Almighty bless you if I never see your face. I love you.

The next year, our family went to a different school. We still had a long walk, and a bull was still chasing us every morning on our way to school. This school was larger. There were more students, and this sometimes made it less friendly. I remember at recess, we were playing baseball, and the bat slipped out of the hand of the batter and struck a girl in the stomach. The girl doubled over in pain for quite some time. She eventually got over it and continued to play baseball. Everyone was trying to console her when she was hurt. I remember thinking that it was nice of everyone to be so concerned, but this type of caring for one another changed when the numbers increased in the school. The increase in the number of students brought on more teachers, hot lunches, and an occasional visit from my dad.

One day a week, the teachers would choose two students to work in the cafeteria. The school now employed a cook who prepared hot meals every day. The water the school used was well water; we enjoyed being picked to bring in the water. It brought forth the opportunity to get out of class a little bit early. It made you feel really special to be singled out for a job. My dad would sometimes come to the school to help bring in wood or get the water needed for lunch. I liked when he came to the school as it gave me the freedom to be outside with him. I could eat any food I wanted to devour. Because Dad was working there, I could work beside him, and we picked whatever we wanted from the school menu.

This school was no different when it came to recess and the games we played. I'm sure it is because we did not have the playground equipment that the other school had, which is why we played such primitive games. I recalled playing a game called war in which we would pick up objects and throw it at an opposing team member. Teams were divided in two groups of fifteen students; we would throw rocks, bricks, or any object we picked up from the ground. One day, while playing this game, a boy picked up a chicken bone and hit a student in the eye. This boy, too, lost his eye just like the other boy did at my previous school. This school was different in the fact that the children seemed violent and out of control. I remember when a ten-year-old boy slammed his fist into the back of a nine-year-old girl. The girl, who was small in stature, doubled over into a pretzel-like shape. The two kids were from different sides of the town. All the kids from the girl's side of town started to run after the boy with nothing but vengeance on their minds. The chase was short; the members of the girl's camp pulverized the young boy. This type of violence brought on a family meeting at the school. The parents had to bring their children, and we all sat and discussed the problem at his school.

So we began to focus on other things to make our free-time productive, or so we thought it to be productive. We started boxing and wrestling. I was so proud of myself in this area. I could control anyone in my age group. I looked forward to my matches. I wasn't a violent boy; I believe it was the competitive spirit that kept me engaged, and the fact that I was tall and muscular. I was such a fierce competitor that one day during one of my matches, a second boy came from behind and pulled my leg from under me. The boy I was wrestling with fell down on top of me, and I hurt my back. The pain jolted down my back with such intense sharpness I believed my back was broken, but to my surprise, after a few short moments, the pain subsided and I was back wrestling. This gave me the unspoken macho attitude that I developed that year. I was a wrestling machine, pinning everyone and loving the fact that I was able to. My youngest son wrestled in high school, and I always smiled to myself knowing where he got all his great moves.

I can remember getting hurt at one of my wrestling matches. At one match, I fell into a hole, and the boy I was wrestling with fell on top of my ankle. He sprung my ankle, and I could not walk well enough to get home. Some friends carried me home, and I was thankful for their show of kindness. When I got home, my parents got a cardboard box and sat me in; I could scoot around the house in it. I was in this predicament for six weeks. I was out of school for the entire time. It was a way of life for people who hurt themselves back then to seek out medical help from family members and not go to a doctor. I can remember hurting myself while riding through the woods on my horse. The horse ran between two trees, and I hit my leg on one of the trees. As I reflect, I know that my leg was probably fractured, but I never went to the doctor or nurse. My parents treated me at home until I got better.

CHAPTER SEVEN

Joined Church

In comparing my childhood to the way that I observe children to be today, I feel like I had a good childhood. I had a wonderful mother and father who knew the importance of childhood. They understood that children needed to grow mentally, physically, spiritually, and emotionally. I was able to explore my surroundings and ask questions and have them answered in a loving and caring way. I enjoyed learning about the different animals, birds, and insects in the woods; I enjoyed exploring, the flowers and plant life, and climbing the trees. I learned about the importance of family—what being in a family really meant. I understand now that family is defined by our commitment, love, and patience, not the blood running through our veins. I learned how to pray to God for each concern in my life and the concerns of others. This is what I have passed to my heritage, and I am very delighted to see that they did get about 60 percent of what family really is all about. The Bible states that we should "train a child when he is young and when he is old he will not depart from it."

Love is the key to family, along with sharing and caring. This was demonstrated to me daily. I can remember my dad's mother sending my sisters and me a box of clothing. Remember, clothing back then consisted of a couple of items and a church outfit. The box contained dresses, pants, and my first suit—the first suit that I ever owned. I love her to this day for her show of kindness and love. I could not wait to go to church that Sunday; I wanted everyone to see my new suit. I got up early and got dressed for Sunday school and church. The walk was miles, but for some reason, that did not bother me at all. My sisters and I walked and talked all the way there, and we had a very nice time that Sunday. The new clothes contributed to the happiness that we felt that day. On our way home, we laughed and played; and when I tried to get through the wire fence in our path, I ripped my suit.

My Walk with Christ

When I was nine years old, I was baptized. My sister and I were baptized on a bright, sunny Sunday morning. The church we attended was the First Baptist Church in Fluker, Louisiana. My pastor was the Honorable Rev. Beacom. He was a great speaker, and I respected him a lot. My sister and I were baptized in a river called Black Creek River. It was such a wonderful experience, and I will always remember that beautiful day. The birds seemed to chirp loudly as if applauding me for coming into the wonderful kingdom of God. The preacher asked us if we believed God raised Jesus from the dead. We replied "yes." He asked us if we believed that Jesus is coming back a second time to reclaim the church. We again said "yes." Then he baptized us in the name of the Father, the name of the Son, and the name of the Holy Ghost. Then he let us go under the water, and when we came up, he said, "Amen." I had always believed in God and Jesus Christ because my family raised us on the principles of the Bible and the Bible teachings. We always went to church and studied the Bible. That was just our way of life. I have always served God and will continue to serve him until the end; that will be my style of life. Afterward, my dad told me that I would have to make righteous decisions from this point on. I began to grow and think more like a young adult rather than a little boy of nine years old. I took my baptism seriously; now I was a Christian.

At school, I had girlfriends; but after my transformation into the spiritual life, I had to choose just one. I could not have five girlfriends and keep lying to them about being faithful. So I chose one—a girl named Amy. Amy had jet—black hair and the whitest teeth I had ever seen. She was a pretty girl, but that was not the reason I decided that she was the one. I liked the way Amy ran; she was the fastest girl in school. If we had had a track team at our school, she would have been a standout in track. I loved when the girls would line up for a race. I was always bragging about how Amy would win the race, and she always won. Amy seemed to like me too; we would pass notes throughout the school day and talk constantly about everything. The best part of our relationship was that we were able to see each other after school too. Her brother and I were good friends, so I would go over his house, and no one was the wiser that she and I were dating. I would hold her hand, and when I left, I would kiss her. That was a big thing back in those days. I was a big shot at school because when the other students heard that I went to her house, they looked up to me as being cool. Sometimes she and I would go in a room alone and kiss for long time. The romance ended when my family moved again. This move was to a town called Hammond, Louisiana.

The Move to Hammond

We moved to a town called Hammond in 1942, still in the state of Louisiana but twenty miles away from Fluker. This move was different because we relocated by horse and wagon. This move of twenty miles took us about six hours to get to our new location. We moved into a pretty sturdy house that had four bedrooms. The bathroom was located outside, and the well water was a half-mile away from the house. I was used to walking for water because, in those days, everyone did unless you were wealthy; both white and black people had to go and get their water from the well. The well was always located on the outside of the house; the toilet was located on the outside too. The folks back in those days considered an inside toilet one of the biggest luxuries around.

A white man, whom my dad knew, owned the house. My dad had made arrangements for him to pay the man $120 dollars a year. The house was on a big farm where my Dad would pick strawberries for the owners. The farm was on twenty acres of land. It had magnificent trees on the land; the trees seemed to be able to reach the sky. I enjoyed looking up and imagining climbing to the very top until I could only see the bright blue sky. I also enjoyed this place because we were able to see the road from where we lived. I could sit on a stoop and see the trucks, wagons, and people pass by. There also was a business next to the property, and several people worked at the car shop. They would work on cars—mainly if there was a problem with the car tires, they would repair the tires. Yes, I really liked the new town we moved to. At this time, I also had a new family member. My youngest brother, Leo, was one at the time. He and I spent hours playing together each day. I was glad that he was born because it meant that I was no longer referred to as the baby.

Another reason that I knew I would like Hammond was the wonderful, friendly neighbor who lived close by us. There was this black man that lived about half a mile from us. He was very nice and did not mind us stopping by his house. He seemed to like the younger generation; he was fifty years old, but his wife was around twenty. They would visit our house, and we would return the favor. His wife was so nice; she would play games with us and bake sweet potatoes for us to eat. Her husband worked for the tire shop, and he also had the job of cutting the grass for the shop. The man who owned the tire shop had a large home with over fifteen large rooms. I knew about the man's house because my mom would clean the rooms, and she also did their laundry. In this city, my mom and dad would work at different places for extra money.

CHAPTER EIGHT

Met Wife in School

The first day of school in Hammond was different from my old school in Fluker. The school was located in a church located on the Old Baton Rouge Highway. The Old Baton Rouge Highway is the name of a street. It sounded like a place rather than the name of a street. The building was bigger than my last school, and the number of students was a lot larger. I can recall how, upon entering the building, I hesitated at the entrance thinking that my new teacher would greet me, welcoming me to my new school. At my old school, the teacher would always welcome new students to the school and make a fuss over the new student. The teacher would go over rules and expectations. The new student was equipped with knowing exactly what was expected from him. This school was different. No one gave me rules, and no teacher greeted me except to order all students to have a seat. I believe it was because Hammond, at the time, was considerably bigger than Fluker. The schoolteachers had more students to teach and were anxious to get to teaching. I believed that was too bad because I believed that they missed the larger picture.

Even though the teacher's congeniality was a little rusty, the students all welcomed me with open arms. They all talked with me at recess wanting to know all about me. I felt really accepted, and I was very grateful. I think they were honest in their actions, but I can't help but wonder if my size played a part in their being too friendly. I was the second-largest student in the building. Working on the farm had given me a muscular body, and my parents' genes had given me pronounced height. There were about thirty-five students in my class, and they were all nice. I had the choice of any girl I wanted to be my girlfriend. The long-distance romance between Amy and me faded rapidly; there was no way to communicate with her, and frankly, I had no emotional ties. I went to school at the church for two years and, after graduating, attended Hammond High School.

High school was a different place, a different type of experience—as I suppose it still is today. The high school was five and a half miles from my home, but the district had provided a bus. This was new to me because I never rode on a school bus; I always walked to school no matter how far away it was located. I liked riding the school bus; it was interesting observing the bus driver stop to pick up kids. I got to see a lot of students and make a lot of friends. After arriving at the school, we went to our homeroom. The teacher was nice but not friendly. All my other classes were in different rooms with different teachers. They too were not friendly. It all seemed like a business; the teachers taught the subject and then moved us on to the next class. It reminded me of when I was at work on the farm, how we would move cattle from one location to another. The one good thing about all the moving was that I met friends galore; I would have a buddy to talk with in every class period and catch up on what was going on around me. I also had my choice of girlfriends, and I dated a lot. It was just easier because of the size of the school.

One day while my friends and I were standing outside waiting for the bus to come, I noticed a very beautiful black girl with shimmering coal-black hair falling down her back. Her hair was braided in three braids,—two in the back and one on top. I loved how she looked so determined, so in-charge, and so beautiful. I did not know her, but the guys I was with knew her family. One guy said to me, "Do you see those kids behind her? Touch one of them, and she will hurt you." I immediately looked behind her, and there were four children who were marching in step behind her. I was so captivated by her I did not notice them before. I also noticed how young they all looked, so I just admired her from afar knowing I was too old to even think about pursuing her as a prospected girlfriend. I did find out that her name was Novella Jones.

School was getting boring for me, and a lot of my friends had left. They went to the military or to work so they could help out the family. I decided to do the same, so after two years of high school, I dropped out and went to work at a box factory.

CHAPTER NINE

First Job

I started working at a factory where they made boxes, all types and sizes. My pay was fifty cents an hour, or twenty dollars a week. I was glad to be able to help my family out financially and help my sister finish her education. I had to push my age up to eighteen to be at the legal work age. I stayed at the factory for two years making the same amount of money; I did not see a raise coming anytime soon. The black men in the South were often overlooked for promotions and raises. A better-paying job was offered to me where I would be making ten dollars more a week. I did not need to be convinced that I should take the job, especially when I deduced that I was not going to move up at the box factory. After leaving the factory, I started becoming restless in the pursuit of a job. I only worked on the new job for three months. Afterward, I moved to my next job at the railroad in Kenner, Louisiana. All these jobs did not last long, about four months was the time limit I seemed to be at for employment.

Some bosses were good, others were not so good. I remember one boss who would scream and use profanity toward his workers. I knew I could not work for him for too long of a time; I was not going to work for someone who mistreated people. I know that the one thing that hurt me the most was not having a high school diploma. I remember going to Baton Rouge and applying at several jobs, but they all said that I needed that diploma in order for me to be hired. There was one position I wanted desperately—it was a job as a bus driver. I wanted that job because the pay was good, and they wore uniforms. I liked to look neat in my appearance, and this job was the one. I just knew this was the job for me. After filling out my application, an employer took me aside. He was a big guy with a twinkle in his eye that made me trust him immediately. He told me that the application was fine, but he could not hire me without the diploma. This made me very despondent, so for a while, I just stopped applying for jobs. I would hang out on the street corners with my friends, and we would talk about all types of things.

We never talked about things too close to home—things such as being black or not having a high school diploma. We would talk about things that made us laugh and forget our status in the South as a black man. In the South, in those times, black men normally did physical labor. If they were not in the fields picking strawberries or some other staple, they were in service jobs such as dishwashers, waiters, bellboys, and jobs that their white counterparts felt comfortable with seeing them doing. For me, the best jobs back in the forties were factory and transportation positions. I just wanted to work to help out the family like so many of my friends. One day, something happened that changed my life. I received a letter from the army stating that I was to report to a certain address to take an exam. I was completely surprised by the letter because I did not talk to a recruiter or go into a military office and apply to join. I was surprised, but I also was smart enough to now that when an official letter like that comes to your house, it is not to be ignored.

Military Life

When I arrived at the office, I was glad to see so many other men at the building. I felt at ease knowing that I would not be taking the physical by myself. I wondered how long it would take for them to contact me after my exam and let me know if my health was good enough to join the army. When I left home, I kissed my mom and told her I probably would be back by lunchtime, but looking at all the long lines of men, I doubted that I would have that lunch date with her.

The man called my number, and I went up to his desk. He was a short, stocky white man who had a raspy voice as though he smoked too many cigars or something. I felt at ease with him because he was friendly and seemed to like me because he was smiling with his eyes. I approached his desk, and he said, "Leroy, go sit on the bench over there." He pointed to an area that was sparsely filled with civilians. After he pointed at the area, I walked over and took a seat. I expected that they got the results and were going to talk with me about them. The man then made the announcement that changed my life immediately.

The man said, "Everybody's names I call, go and sit beside Leroy Walls because you are in the army!"

I heard his words, but I don't think they registered in my brain. *What was he talking about? What did he say?* All types of questions exploded in my head. This was not what I was expecting when I woke up this morning. My thoughts raced back to home. I could see Mom baking the corn bread for our lunch. I could feel the dismay she would feel when she thought I was running late and maybe forgetting about our lunch together; I knew she had questions to ask about my coming to this office. The worst part of all this was that my mom's anger would turn into fear when I did not return home that night. I felt helpless and a bit annoyed that the army would do this without giving me a chance to say good-bye to my family. My family would worry about me because so many young black men back then went missing and were never found, or worse, were found dead. I was glad, however, that I spoke with mom that morning before coming, and she knew where I was going. My mom, being as smart as she was, would deduce what happened to me. I'm sure it would take her a while to put it all together because the last time she and I spoke, I was going to the military office to take a test. Too bad that neither we nor anyone we knew had a phone back then. I'm sure that they would have allowed us to call home.

I was bused off to a place called Fort Hood, Texas, for training. At first, it was very hard for me because I refused to do a lot of what I was told to do. I believe it was because of the way I got into the army; I felt as if I had been tricked and lied to. After my basic training, I remained in Texas because all recruits that did not have a high school diploma were required to go back to school and get one. That was where the blessing came in. The army provided me with the opportunity to get my education. My entire attitude changed, and I began to appreciate and like the army.

After my training, I was sent to Korea, and on an experience that I will always remember. I had only traveled to Texas as a child, but now I would be going to another country. The trip started at Washington, DC, we boarded a ship that seemed bigger than any land monument that I knew of. The ship had all kinds of different areas, just like being in a building on land. There were so many servicemen doing various jobs on the ship. When we boarded the ship, I could not tell that we were on water. Our commander lectured us about becoming seasick and how normal that was if we experienced it. He also advised us to keep food in our stomachs as that would help ease some of the seasickness. Then we went to our bunks, and the ship started sailing for Japan. The journey took fifteen days to get from Washington to Japan. The first three days, I was sick and spent a lot of time throwing up. My fellow recruits shared this act. After fifteen days, we finally arrived in Japan but were told we had to remain on the ship. I suppose that they didn't want us to get used to being on land and start with the seasickness all over again. The rest of the voyage lasted two more days, and then we were in Korea.

Korea was different! The people, the food, and the language—the entire culture—was so different from what I was used to. Fish was the main food in Korea; they loved to eat fish heads and rice. The rice was grown in large fields all over the country. I use to love rice until I witnessed how it was fertilized in Korea. The people would use their waste for fertilization, and that, to me, was not acceptable. When it was hot outside, the entire city would reek with the smell of waste. The smell reminded me of a big bathroom that had feces in the toilet bowl. I had a hard time eating rice, even when I returned to the United States.

The people seemed friendly enough, but the communication was an obstacle. The army gave us books with the most commonly used words in our language and the translated version in their language. I knew the basic words like *hello, it, money, help, what,* etc., words that could get me through the day when dealing with the people of the country. A lot of the population could speak English reasonably well; they referred to us as "GI." The children were always asking for change; we did not mind giving our change to the little ones, especially since a lot of the soldiers had children at home, and the kids may have reminded them of their own families. The citizens were friendly, but some were known to be thieves. The misconception was that we Americans were all well off, so there were some individuals who wanted to share in our wealth. I recall one day just walking from my station and running across a young man around my age who seemed like he wanted to walk with me and talk. My Korean language was limited, but I knew enough of the language to hold a decent conversation. The guy understood English a little bit too. We were doing fine until I felt him trying to steal my wallet, which was dumb because I had a .45 at my waist. I pulled my gun out and pointed it at him, and he could speak English well. He kept repeating for me not to shoot him and professing to be sorry for what he tried to do.

My job in the military was to ride on the tank as an assistant driver. I was assigned to the twenty-fourth division; it was a very nice company. There were five men on the tank along with the big gun. This gun was amazing to me; I had been around guns all my life but none was even close to this one. This gun could hit a target eleven miles away. I was glad to be riding on the tank when so many other guys were walking or riding on trucks. We were never in danger because this was peacetime; there was no war going on. I even went to North Korea. The United States' side was South Korea, but my commander had me drive to North Korea because he had a package to pick up. The trip was easy until we were on our way back to the south side. We were driving down a hill and the jeep quit. The jeep was headed in a downward motion, so I just let the jeep coast around and around the hill all the way to the bottom. The hill was around an eight-hundred-foot drop, so I held the stirring wheel tightly. I was a bit scared but determined not to show it. We got down the hill safely.

One commonality that the Koreans share with the United States is their belief in God. I asked the locals about what God they served, and they told me that they served the God in the Bible. I ask a few but was sure there were other religions over there. I went to a church service and was surprised to see the people shouting all over the church. I was happy to see that they served God. The military was a good experience for me. I've talked with guys who had negative comments about their experience in the military. I can only say that I'm sorry for their bad experiences, but that just is not my story. The military gave me the opportunity to travel, finish my education, and a have a job all at the same time. In the South, for a black man, that was a lot of accomplishments. The best part of being in the military and away from the States was receiving mail. The mail call was the most popular event on the base. Everyone showed up when it was time for mail to be distributed. We longed for our names to be called and get a letter from someone back home. I enjoyed all the mail I received from friends and family, but my biggest desire was to get the letters from my beautiful Novella. She and I started dating three years after seeing her with her siblings that day after school. I saw her again three years later, and we started dating before I left for Korea. I really looked forward to her letters because I was able to really express all my emotions in my letters, and she did the same. I knew in my heart that she was the one for me, and I hoped she felt the same. After mail call, most guys would go back to their tent to sleep, listen to the radio, or play cards for the rest of the evening. I was glad that it was peacetime and that the war was over when I arrived in Korea. I had the pleasure to go all around the area without the fear of being attacked. Prior to my coming to this country, the north side had fought against the south side. The United States was on the side of South Korea, and Russia was on the side of North Korea, but now it was peacetime, and I could travel across the frontline.

CHAPTER TEN

Joined the Army

After being in South Korea for one year, I returned to the United States. We traveled on the ship again for fifteen days, but this time, there was a train ride added for three days, and then a taxi for a day, and my final mode of transportation was a bus. When the bus stopped in Hammond, what a beautiful sight waiting for me—there was my girlfriend just as pretty as a picture standing there to greet me. I did not think it possible for her to get prettier than she already was, but somehow she accomplished that.

After seeing her, I thought back to when I first saw her that day after school while standing on the corner with my friends. I remember how her beauty stood out like a picture painted by some great artist. Her beauty was not like some of the girls I knew that had painted what they felt beauty should look like on their faces; her beauty was all-natural, as if she could wake up and not even worry about looking into a mirror. She captivated me the first time I saw her, but at that time, she was only nine years old, and I was thirteen. I saw her as a little girl. I could not think of her as a girlfriend because I had just started school there after my move from Fluker. I couldn't be seen talking to a child. I was popular on campus and could date any girl I wanted. I dated others, but Novella was the one in my heart. We stated dating later, and now there she was, standing at the bus stop looking like an angel.

After I talked with Novella for a long time, I caught another cab to go home to my family. They were all so happy to see me, and I felt the same way. Mom had prepared all my favorite dishes, and I ate like there was no tomorrow. I then went to my bedroom and went to sleep. I did not wake up until the next evening. While being alone and pondering about life, God gave me a revelation. Life is what you make of it, not what others make of it for you. I began to see life and what life was all about; it is just what you make out of it—good or bad, it is all up to you. So I began to look at my future. The army gave me a three-year scholarship, which I used to get my high school diploma. My mother had saved the money I sent home from my military pay, which amounted to $400. That was a lot of money back in the fifties. Mom used what money she needed for bills and living costs and put the rest in the bank for me for when I got out. I bought a car, and I put $150 down and made monthly payments until I paid the $500 that the car cost. I also bought an acre of land in Rose Hill Park, paying $10 month until the $400 was paid in full. Novella and I were married, and God blessed us with three children. We were very happy.

After being married for almost eight years, my wife and I decided to move up north.

CHAPTER ELEVEN

Northward Bound

I had been married for ten years. The year was 1966. I had three children, and the wife and I decided to move to the North. At first we talked about Texas, a place where my father was born, and those nice vacations I took as a child. I remember all the life lessons I was taught there. Texas was very high on the list of places to move to. Another state that the wife and I considered was California. I had a lot of friends who moved west, and they seemed to have made the transition smoothly. I had family in Texas and friends in California, so both places seemed like a great place to live and raise a family. I loved the Texas weather, so that was a point for Texas, but my lovely wife reminded me that the weather in California was just as nice. We debated back and forth on where we would move to, but that was all we did at that time. We did not have any great need to move because God had blessed us abundantly right where we were, but an incident happened that pushed me to do more than just talk about moving.

I was working at the brickyard in Baptist, Louisiana. We had about eighty or ninety employees. We had a union, something that was not that popular back in the sixties. I was elected union steward. A union steward was the employee who was chosen to make sure that rules and regulations were being followed properly. The position only required two stewards, which was, again, a nice position to be in because you could negotiate and monitor the employer's behaviors and also seek higher wages for your coworkers. Of course, with that being said, you can imagine that the owners of the business did not want a union, and believe it or not, some of the workers did not want the union to come in. It was a misguided belief that the union would cause problems and possibly cost some job loss. Remember, this was in the sixties and in the South, so a lot of workers did not want to rock the boat. They just wanted to work and go home; as long as they had money coming in, they did not care if they were made to work twelve hours a day for minimum pay.

The majority won and our union was up and going. All was going well on the job, and we were very happy with what the union represented for us. My job was to haul dope from the work site to various places. Sometimes my position with the company would take me miles away from home. I had an assignment that took me ten miles away from the site. When I returned from the site, all the employees were out on strike. They were angry because a supervisor kicked an employee about his dog. I drove the truck onto the property, and no one was working. I asked, "What is the problem?" They responded that they were on strike due to cruelty to employees, and they asked me what I was going to do about the matter. I told them that the union was not to go on strike without the approval of the union staff and with a majority vote from the employees. I tried to explain to them that there is a process that must be followed in order for the union concept to work. I tired of trying to explain to them how it was supposed to work. I was very glad that it was Friday. I was also glad to be starting my vacation the following week. After trying to explain to my coworkers that what they were doing was illegal, and we would be penalized if they did not return to their work, I went in to see my boss and asked for my pay. I received my regular check along with my vacation check.

My vacation took me to a small northern town called Centralia, Illinois. I decided to go there to see if I could find a job and move from the state of Louisiana. After the union fiasco, I was more determined to go to a place with a different environment and, hopefully, a different mind-set. After getting the go-ahead from my lovely wife, I decided to go forward and try and find another place for my family and me. I decided to visit my cousin Taylor Miller, who lived in Centralia. He and I talked often about relocating to a different area. In the past, he had invited me to come and visit with him and his family. I always said that I would but really never got around to taking the invitation seriously. This was my chance to take advantage of his offer. I would be going alone so I could have the freedom to look for employment without worrying about my wife and children being in a strange place. Another reason I went alone was because my cousin and his wife were going through a divorce. The wife had already moved out, and Taylor was now living alone with his two sons. It was not a happy time for him. As a matter of fact, he was thinking about moving back to Louisiana.

My wife was very supportive because she wanted to move. She often complained about never leaving the state. She was excited about the prospect of moving to the North, East, or West—she just wanted to see a different sight. She also wanted the children to have a better education; she had heard that the education system was top-notch in the north. The idea that her children would be getting a better education was very pleasing to her. That was all the support I needed, so the next day, I went to the train station and bought a ticket to Centralia, Illinois.

Centralia was seven hundred miles away, and I felt that the train ride would give me a lot of time to reflect and figure out where God was leading me. The ride was about fourteen hours long, and I spent a great deal of that time praying that I could find a job and a place for my family to live. I heard a lot about the north and the opportunity that it offered, especially for black people. I heard that there were better living conditions, and the north would allow me to pursue the dreams that I had for my life without any of the jejune Jim Crow laws.

My parents were farmers. They were Christians. My dad was a preacher, and my mom was the mother of the church. That was my life, and that was all I knew. I was not complaining because we had a great life. I was very thankful for the life that my parents offered me, especially with the horror stories that happened to other blacks in the South at that time. I remembered the years in Fluker, Louisiana, and attending the First Baptist Church. I also remembered the move to Hammond where Dad purchased ten acres of land on the Old Baton Rouge Highway about five miles from Hammond. I also went to school at the church that was located on the Old Baton Rouge Highway. That was where I met my wife for the first time. She was a beautiful girl of nine years old, and I was thirteen years old. I recalled us attending Greenville school together. I saw her as a nice girl who took good care of her brother and sisters. The year was 1945, but now I was on the train thinking about what would happen when I reached this new place in the North. The North—the land of great opportunity and new attitudes regarding race. I knew I was willing to work, and I felt that was all I needed to be successful.

When I arrived at the train station in Centralia, Illinois, I was expecting to see my cousin TB (that is what we called him). I regarded him as a big brother, someone I looked up to. He and his first wife, Gladys, lived with my mom and dad in Fluker for a length of time. He moved to Centralia with his second wife, Idela. He had two sons by his second wife and two girls by his first wife. He was a big man with a big round head. I remember how his head always seemed too big for his body.

I talked with TB several times before my trip, and he had warned me about the weather in the north and that it is sometimes very cold. I was arriving in May, so I did not concern myself too much about it being cool, but just in case, I brought a couple of sweaters with me. While looking out the window of the train, I could see the beautiful land as we passed through Mississippi, Tennessee, Arkansas, Kentucky, and, finally, Illinois. The sign read: Land of Lincoln. My mind wandered back to my beautiful family and what they might be doing at this time. We had just built a brand-new home, and everyone was questioning us about trying to leave after just building a new home. They also reminded me about my job and my position with the union. We were getting all kind of opposition about why we should move and not be happy with our lot in life. After all, we had it good. I believe now it was because of the family we would be leaving, and they would miss us for sure. Novella and I would miss them also, but the adventure-seekers in us, the love for our children, and the faith in God kept us moving forward to our move. I thought about the Bible and how others left their homes and families not sure of what was on the other side of the mountain. God told Abraham to go away from his family to a land that he did not know. God told him to walk before him, and he would bless him and his children to the fourth generation if he would obey his word. So Abraham walked as God said, and God blessed Abraham. As I rode the train, I thought about Abraham and his faith in God. I felt that I was not alone in this decision; I knew God was with my family and me wherever we moved to. I hoped for the best and tried to walk and do things the way that I felt were pleasing to God.

As we stopped at the station and I was gathering my belongings, I was anxious for my new adventure. I was not afraid at all. As a matter of fact, I was the complete opposite of afraid. When the train arrived in Centralia, it was very dark outside. I had not noticed from the train that it was now night. I had one suitcase and a bag and a whole lot of optimism. I knew my wife was at home praying for me, praying for us. When I got off the train, I really could not get a clear picture of the town because it was dark, but I felt I would recognize my cousin even in the dark. If I couldn't make out his face, I knew I would recognize his silhouette. He was a big man with big, broad shoulders—something I admired about him when he used to live with us in Louisiana. I looked for him but did not see him anywhere, but I did notice a big man in front of the train cleaning off the windows at the station. He stopped work and started to talk with another man. My cousin was yelling, and that is when I recognized him by his voice. I made the connection in my head; I remembered that my cousin told me that he worked for the railroad. He then noticed me standing by the station's desk and walked toward me with his big smile. His teeth would shine when he smiled because he had that signature Louisiana gold over two of his teeth. The young kids call it bling and think that they started the gold-in-the-mouth phenomenon, but in the South, they were doing it long before some of these entertainers were born.

He greeted me with "Hi, Lee! Glad to see you." I responded with a relieved hello, and he gave me instructions on how to get to his house. He had a few more hours to work and could not leave, but his sons were at the house, and they would let me in. His house was about six blocks away, and I found the walk very nice after being on the train all those hours. When I arrived at his home, his children were there but not his wife. She had left him and went back to live in Louisiana. They were separated. I had no idea that his wife had moved back south.

I was glad to be there but very tired. I had a good night's sleep, and the next day, I was hitting on the search for employment. That morning, I got a good look at Centralia, Illinois. The town was small and old in appearance; it had an antique persona about it. The population was around thirteen thousand people. The town was a small, big town in the sense that there were a lot of businesses in the location and a college. There were five factories, a railroad, and lots of other places one could find employment. I knew God would lead me to a job. Centralia being so small, everyone knew each other, or at least knew of the next person, so when a new person moved to town, the townspeople would find out who they were and where they came from. It was easy for me because my cousin had established himself in the community, so I was accepted as being okay. My cousin was glad to show me the town. We went to several places. I went to the railroad first because that was where he was employed, and it was known for being the best-paying job. It had about two thousand workers; he introduced me to some of the workers and to the supervisor. I put my resume in and hoped that he would call me to work. I also put my resume in a lot of other businesses. That first day was very busy for me. While I was searching looking for employment, I also was looking at schools. My children were young, and I wanted them to have a good education. I had always heard that the educational system in the north was a good one, so I was not too worried about their educational needs being met. I learned that the city was 75 percent white and 25 percent black. It did not matter to me because I had heard that the north was fair in their hiring, education, and pay.

CHAPTER TWELVE

Sharecropper's Son in the North

On Sunday morning, we all went to church. It was a Baptist church and had about sixty-five members. The church had a brilliant choir, mostly because of the piano player. She was phenomenal. After service, I was introduced to the members. They all welcomed me and wanted me to talk about where I was from. I also talked with members about employment in the city. I knew that networking could help me find employment. To my dismay, most of the members said that the town had little employment openings and that if I relocated there, it would be difficult for me to find housing. I didn't get discouraged because I believed my fate was in the hands of a higher power.

On Monday morning, I set out to look for work. I remember being glad that the town was so small, and I could walk anywhere in the city without working up a good sweat. The many years of being a sharecropper's son had built my body up to accept walking miles as a common thing. By the end of the week, I had several phone calls for employment. Three of the businesses offered me a job. I was glad that I got an offer; I felt that God was guiding me to move to Illinois. I accepted a job as a welder at a place that made air-conditioners and heaters. The company was called Ziegler's; it was a big employer of the people in the community. The company had about five hundred employees. The supervisor talked with me about my future with the company, and I enjoyed what he had to say. In the South, I never had a supervisor sit down with me and discuss my future. This was all new, but I liked it. The supervisor told me that he was going to train me for a special position with the company. I was very happy with all the supervisor had presented to me. I felt as though this was the perfect time to tell him about my own plans. I shared with him my plans to relocate and how I would need time to move my family up north. We discussed my plans, and he agreed that I would work for a week and then leave for Louisiana to bring my family back with me.

My cousin was happy that I found a job and would be moving to the north. He was very happy because he felt lonely after his wife left him. So when we went to church that Sunday, I proudly shared with the church that I had, in fact, gotten a job. I looked around at all the ones who said that there were no jobs in the town. I know that is why the Bible tells us not to put our faith in man but to put our faith and trust in him. The men in the church seemed happy that I did not listen to them. After service, I called my wife and told her to pack for the move. She was happy but wanted to know where we would be staying. I told my cousin that my family would be looking for an apartment and asked where we could find one that fits our family needs. He suggested that we rent from him. He owned a two-story house and said that he and his boys were the only ones staying there since his wife left. He offered us a part of the house to live in until we found a place suitable for us to live in. We rented out three rooms upstairs, and we paid half of the utilities. TB wanted me to wait to start paying on our arrangements, but I refused because I always believed in paying my way. I believe that was the only fair way to make it all work, so we agreed upon those terms.

After two weeks, I was on my way back to Louisiana from Illinois. I talked to Novella on the phone again, and she told me she was packed and ready for the move. That is why I love this lady. She is always my biggest encourager; she always did and still does stick beside me like glue. I love her dearly. I had been away from her and the children for two weeks, but it seemed like six months. I was so glad to be going back to my family. When I got on the train, I spotted what I thought was an empty seat and sat down feeling full of energy. After I was seated, an older woman came and sat down beside me. She had been in the restroom. She said to me, "Hello, young man." I greeted her back. She proceeded to tell me that she came all the way from Chicago, and no one sat in the seat I now sat in beside her, so she saw our union as a sign from God. She was on her way to Memphis, Tennessee. The lady had a job where she worked with teachers; she advised them about what they were presenting in the classroom. She advised them as an attorney would do. I'm sure that her position was a powerful one.

She asked me how far I was going, and I told her my destination. She was a well-educated lady, I could tell by our conversation, and she was a lady who told about things that were to happen in the future.

Born and raised in Louisiana, I had heard about people like her—people who were able to predict the future. Some said that they could, others said that they could not. I always took everything to the Bible for confirmation on any subject. I did not concern myself with whether she was a fortune-teller or a prophetess, all I knew was that I was really enjoying her conversation and company.

After I revealed to her that I was going to get my family so that we could move to Louisiana, she talked about different subjects. We talked about world affairs—at that time, a lot was being discussed in the news about Dr. Martin Luther King and the Kennedy brothers. We talked about our views on what they were doing for the country. We talked for hours, and soon I began to feel as if she was a friend rather than a stranger. She turned the conversation toward my family. At the time, I had three children, two boys and one girl. She told me that I had a nice family. She told me that my oldest son was going to have a business when he grew up. She said that my daughter had a good eye for clothing and to let her pick out her own clothes. She told me that my baby son was going to be good for the community and that maybe he should be a pharmacist. I was glad that she said positive things about my children. My last son was not born yet; he would be born up north. She also talked about my wife and me. She told me that my job required me to wear a robe, and to my surprise, she was right. I was the choir director at my church, and I had to wear a robe for the job. I told her about my position in the church, and she and I laughed and kept on talking. She also told me that my wife would like Illinois at first but, later, will not enjoy the state because of hard times that would occur. She told me to tell my wife to save her money and to work hard. To my surprise, she even told me about my cousin, Taylor. She said that "he was getting ready to move back south until you decided to come north," that he was depressed because his wife had left him, and he felt alone. She also gave me some Bible verses to give to him to read; she felt that the scriptures would help him in his depressed state of mind. This lady is part of my story because of our conversation, and more often than not, a lot of the things she was saying were true. One statement she made really got my attention. She told me that my mother had passed away, and a lot of other things in my life that were true. I remembered thinking, *How could she know these things?*

The train traveled steadily down the tracks, and before we knew it, the conductor was shouting that we were approaching Memphis, Tennessee. I help her with her bags for her departure. She looked me directly in the eye and said to me, "Make sure that you take some gifts to your children, something to show that you were thinking about them. It could be candy or a toy." I walked her to the end of the train aisle. The lady with her wide smile and great conversation looked back at me before stepping onto the steps that the conductor put out for her and said, "Good luck, young man." She then placed fifty cents in my hand. I opened my hand and looked again to thank her, but she had gone into the crowd. I walked back to my seat pondering over our conversation and thinking how rich it was for me, and I hoped for her too. The rest of the train ride, I slept and dreamed of my wife waiting at the station for me. I could see her, ebony-colored skin and her raven-dark hair neatly pressed, looking up at the train trying to seek me out. I could not help but thank God for my life at this point. He guided me in the direction that my heart desired; I wanted a change in my environment, and he granted my request. I was going to Illinois to live there. So when the train pulled into the station of Hammond, I was happy to see my wife waiting for me, looking just like I had imagined. She told me all that had happened while I was away. She said that she was ready to move because she had lived in Louisiana all her life. On the way home, we stopped at the store for three boxes of Cracker Jacks to give to the children. I wanted them to have a little gift from me to let them know that I was thinking about them while I was away. On the way home, I told my wife about my train ride back to Illinois.

While we were packing and preparing for our move, I was surprised at how many family members and friends were not in agreement with our decision to move. We had family telling us discouraging stories about why we should not move north. My brother-in-law reported to me that life was hard up north, and he knew of families moving up north and returning home within two years. Friends of mine were trying to convince me of the foolishness of our move and reminding us that we had just built a brand-new house. That was the biggest argument of all about our decision to relocate. We had our home built from the ground up on one acre of rich farmland. We went to New Orleans and purchased furniture to put in our new home. We had a brand-new car that we bought a year ago, so we were living very well at the time.

The opposition continued to come in from friends and family, but Novella and I continued to pack. There is a saying that goes "when you move, you lose," and it is true. We left a lot, but we were looking forward to the future. We both knew that we could get everything and more back if we continue to follow God and serve him. That was and still is our answer to everything. We told family members and friends that God is everywhere, and he would be with us in Illinois just as he is with us in Louisiana. I knew we did know a lot of people in Illinois, but I felt that we could make new friends. The one thing I was certain of was that Jesus would be with us. My daily prayer would be for God to lead my family in the way that would be pleasing in his sight.

CHAPTER THIRTEEN

On the Road

My wife and I loaded the children for our road trip to the north. The children were wide-eyed, excited, and fearless in the backseat of our new blue Pontiac. We knew the trip would take a while because Louisiana was about seven hundred miles from Illinois, and with the children needing to stop, I figured that would add an extra two hours. The year was 1966, and we would not be returning to live in this state again until the next century.

We decided to travel down Highway 51 because they were working on Highway 55. I could have taken Highway 55 for part of our trip, but I felt the slow and steady pace would give my children more of the sights to observe. I also, at the time, felt a little safer traveling down a highway I was more familiar with driving on.

When we started out, the children were in the backseat asleep, and my beautiful Novella was next to me. I started to think about the conversation that I had on the train with the lady and about my new job. It was a nice day for traveling; I started out early because I knew my children would be sleeping for a large portion of the trip. We left our house around four o'clock in the morning, and it was still dark outside. The children were awake for only a few minutes, and then their wide eyes closed again into a deep sleep. I decided that this was all in God's plan because we were headed north.

I played the radio quietly to keep me from falling asleep and, really, to have sound in the car. I liked listening to talk radio especially at this time in history because the country was full of race problems. I was looking forward to the move to the north because I had hopes that race issues would not be an issue in Centralia. I thought about how the slaves were always trying to reach the north to find states where slavery was not accepted. My feelings were that we were now in the sixties, so the northern states must have advanced even further when it came to their intolerance of prejudice. On the radio, the radio host was talking about how blacks were marching through the streets in protest of Jim Crow laws. The relationship between blacks and whites had been one of cruelty. Whites were being cruel to black folks, and blacks were being cruel to white folks. Of course, not all people were cruel to each other because some people knew the true words of Jesus. He taught us that we should love each other. Those of us who have Christ on our hearts could never be cruel to another human because of his or her skin color.

On our journey through Mississippi, it was about nine thirty when I decided to get more gas. We pulled into the station, and I filled my car up. The children started to wake up, and my daughter, Shari, said, "Dad, I want a cold drink." I noticed a Coke machine on the outside of the station and a man standing beside the machine enjoying his coke. I went to the machine, but there was a sign on it that said the machine was out of order. I told the man standing by the machine that my children wanted a drink and that I'd like to get one from the machine if possible.

He looked at me, then at my car, and said in almost a snarl, "The machine is broken."

I said to him, "You are drinking a cold drink where did you get yours from?"

At this time, we must have been getting loud (although I didn't think my voice was rising) because my wife yelled my name. "Lee! Let's go."

I got the message; the man did not want to let blacks get a drink at his place. It was okay for blacks to spend their money on gas at his station—after all, money is green—but as far as getting a drink or food at his station, that was not going to happen. The law may say that his antics were illegal, but who could prove that his ridiculous practices were illegal? If that little incident was not enough to make me want to run to the north, the next stop did.

Our next stop was even worse because we had the displeasure of dealing with an individual who was a complete idiot. We made another stop because my baby girl wanted a drink. Novella and I felt it safe to stop in another state. Memphis was the next state, so we decided to stop and stretch our legs and get my baby her drink. I started to pump the gas while the family went inside to get some refreshments. After I pumped the gas, I went inside to join them. The person behind the counter was so rude and nasty. His tone let Novella and I know that we were not welcome in his store, but of course, the green money was welcomed. We exchanged looks as we walked slowly to the car. We were both thinking the same thing.

The children did not notice any thing out of the ordinary. My wife and I made sure that we sheltered them from all the ugliness that we possibly could keep away from their young lives. When I would look at them playing, laughing, and singing church songs, I always thanked God for their happiness. One of my fondest memories of our trip was when the kids were in the backseat singing songs they learned in church. I can remember the words of one song that they sung in the backseat.

What you gonna do when the world's on fire? Where you gonna run? Where you gonna run? I ain't gonna run. I'm stand right here. I'm gonna ask the Lord, "Don't let the fire do me no harm because I've been dipped in the water" . . . a boom boom da boom.

They sang that song practically through the entire state of Arkansas. I remember thinking about those rude looks that we got in Tennessee at the gas station and thought that they should hear my children sing that song. I was glad that the children were in good spirits, and I was glad at that moment to be taking them to a place where they would not be judged by the color of their skin.

We continued our journey, and Novella decided to drive for a while. I was more than happy to get out from under the wheel. This would give me a chance to relax and see the sights that we had on both sides of the highway. So we continued to travel down Highway 51. On this route, you would pass through every town. In some places, we did have to detour to Interstate 55, but we always managed to get back on our Highway 51 and remained on it for the seven-hundred-mile trip.

We stopped at parks and let the children run and play. They seemed to love running around and taking in all the sights. There were so many fruit trees along the way, and my children were full of questions about the fruit, birds, etc. As we entered the state of Illinois, my wife was doing a great job with the driving. She normally drove a little too fast for my taste, but this time, she was driving at a comfortable speed. My relaxation came to a halt when we came to a place where construction workers were working on the road ahead of us. The two-lane road turned into a one-lane road, and on either side of the road, you could look down to a ditch that had a fifty-foot drop. My wife could not pull over and let me drive, so she continued on the road. The children seemed to sense that we were in a precarious situation because all singing stopped. The backseat was dead silent, and so was I. This construction went on for ten miles, and the car was silent the entire ten miles. When the construction came to an end, my wife pulled over and said, "Now you can drive." I said okay and got back under the wheel.

The children seemed to breathe better, and I started looking for the first gas station because we were low on gas. We were in a city called Cairo, Illinois; I saw all blacks at one gas station, and all whites at another gas station. I did not know at the time that they were having racial problems. I filled up my tank and proceeded toward Centralia, Illinois. We were only about one hundred miles away from our new town, and I was very optimistic.

The state of Illinois was so beautiful to look at. The sign read: Land of Lincoln. I thought about the family taking a trip one day to visit his tomb in Springfield, Illinois, and we did a year later.

One last rest stop, and we were on our way to our destination. As we approached our new home, I could see some of the places I recognized, some of the places that I had seen when I was there on vacation. I was thankful that we were close to the end of the trip. We pulled up to TB's street and the street we would be living on. TB was our only relative in the town, but he did have his mother's sister living there, and she had children. I had never met her, but I did recall my mother talking about her when I was a child.

As I got closer to the house, a flood of thoughts flashed through my mind like a movie reel out of control. I thought about the new friends my family would encounter, and a poem that my son had to recite for school arose: "What a wonderful thing to know we have friends wherever we go; friends to be with when we are happy, friends to cheer us when we are sad. We have mother, father, sister and brother; for this I'll give my thanks to God."

We were now coming into Centralia; the population was thirteen thousand people, and the town we left had ten thousand people. The numbers were not that different, but what I felt made the biggest difference was that we were seven hundred miles coming from a southern state and entering a northern state. I hoped that the mind-set would be different for my family and me regarding race.

Driving down Cherry Street was impressive; the street was lined with enormous oak trees with branches that draped over the street like a big canopy. The houses were neatly kept with each lawn manicured to the smallest detail. I continued to tell my family about our cousin's house and how it was located at the end of the street. TB had a two-story house that sat on a corner lot. It, like a lot of the houses and buildings in Centralia, was old and historic-looking. That was one of the comments my wife made when we first entered the town. She was looking for newer buildings because we had just left a newly built house that sat on an acre of land. I knew she was a little disappointed, but Novella was not a complainer but a doer. She could make a full-course meal out of flour and water if she needed to.

We finally reached our destination, and I pulled in the driveway. Immediately, Saber, the big German shepherd, started barking and racing back and forth across the driveway. The dog was tied to an oak tree that stood at the far end of the driveway. A massive collar was around his neck that was connected with a chain—this support was all that could hold the dog; any other form of leash would be futile. The teenage boys bounced out on the porch to greet us. They had been expecting our arrival. We all made our introductions, but I could tell by the way that Novella was looking at the house she was disappointed. The porch was old and could use a paint job, and the house was a two-story, but it was leaning at an angle. It is funny how you don't notice imperfections until someone you love points them out to you. In the case of Novella, she didn't complain, but I knew her well enough to read her expressions, especially the ones her eyes revealed. I did not notice before how the door screen was not completely attached to the door. I did not notice how the table, as you entered the house, did not have one cleared-off space on it for a plate to be placed. The house looked pretty cluttered and unkempt, something I did not notice before. Men see order so differently than a woman does. Still, she never orally complained. She wanted to see the upstairs where we would be living. We were so exhausted from the long trip that all we could think about was getting some rest.

I was so caught up in observing Novella that I really did not observe the children and their expressions of their new home. Rodney, my baby boy, could not get over the dog and how big he was; he kept asking questions about Saber. Shari did not seem to show any expression—she was always happy in any given situation. Reggie just looked and seemed to accept his new home.

We headed upstairs to rest, but the children went outside to explore. When I woke up, Novella was outside too. She was excited about TB's garden. He had a small garden that housed about ten rolls, and it covered about fifty feet. Novella loved working in her garden back home. We grew all sorts of vegetables, and we grew strawberries, some we sold to the local markets for a hefty additional income. She found something in our move to get her excited—the garden, which is her way. The woman loved a challenge.

The first day at TB's house, we unloaded the car and checked out our surroundings. From the upstairs window, the view was very nice. We could see all the way downtown, and the area looked friendly enough. The houses were close together, that was clearly a difference from what we were used to. The houses in the South came with a lot of land; neighbors were never as close to each other as they were in the North. Another difference was the race of our neighbors—all of them were Caucasian. What a cultural shock, but after all, we were up north, and the color barriers were down.

Later that day, TB and I talked about our move, and he thanked me for moving to Centralia. He said that he was thinking about moving to Texas or California because he was not happy there anymore. He proceeded to talk about raising his boys and how hard it was for him after she left. He went on to say that he tried hard to live a Christian life but was finding it difficult. I found that so ironic because of the conversation I had with the lady on the train. I told him everything the lady on the train had said about him not being happy because of his wife leaving. I also told him that she was a Christian lady and that she gave me scriptures to give to him so he could read them. He found this all amazing too, and he seemed to be glad to get the scriptures.

That Sunday, we all went to the church as a family. I introduced my family to the congregation, and they responded nicely. The pastor and his wife welcomed them with open arms. That was when I decided that I really liked this church. After visiting other churches, this was the church that gave me a feeling of family. The pastor, Rev. Jesses Beacoat and his wife, Clemaude Mary Beacoat, were warm and friendly people who loved God dearly. The Beacoats were both in their fifties, and they both loved children. Mrs. Beacoat, who was their Sunday-school teacher, taught my children. I took the family to the other churches in town. They enjoyed the visit to New Bethel, Second Baptist, and other churches. I was surprised at the makeup of the congregation. For some reason, I thought that the congregation would be mixed because we were up north. There were no Jim Crow laws, but I still saw blacks attending all-black churches and whites attending all-white churches. I asked my cousin about this situation and if the town had any churches where the congregation was mixed with both black and white. Taylor's response was that anywhere God provided land for the blacks, the whites tried to put the blacks off the land. I pondered on his words and came to a colossal understanding. I realized that it is neither the town nor state that you live in that determines whether or not the area is prejudiced but it is indeed the people who live in that state or city.

I remembered being in Korea and living with a lot of different people, and this experience taught me to observe differences, so I was trying to get a feel of the people I was living among. The next Sunday, my family and I joined Macedonia Baptist Church under Pastor Beacoat. We were happy with our decision because we had family in the church, and Beacoat allowed me to serve as a deacon and choir president just as I did at my old church in Hammond. I was so thankful to be able to step back into those roles in the church. I also had a great relationship with Pastor Beacoat. I would drive him to different churches in Saint Louis and Peoria. Pastor and Mrs. Beacoat were in their fifties, and it was an honor to be able to help them get around. I also developed a relationship as that of a son to him; he reminded me a lot of my dad.

I learned how to get around in the state, which afforded me to know about the historic sites in the state. With this knowledge, I would take my children on minivacations. The children loved the trips. I remember going to a site called Hole in the Rock. The children would run and explore the huge cave-like structure. The one place we all enjoyed was the trip to Lincoln's Tomb; I remember my youngest son climbed the statue of Lincoln and rested on his arm so he could pose better for the picture Novella was taking. We went on lots of fishing trips and picnics. We enjoyed our children and felt that they would always be close. Novella had a sister who lived in the suburbs of Chicago, and we would visit her often.

I was really enjoying my move, especially my work at the church. I was the youngest deacon in the ministries, so the older deacons would help me and give me sound training in my duties. Rev. Beacoat made sure that I was taken care of. He would tell the older deacons to make room for me and help train me. Rev. Beacoat stood about five feet six inches tall and weighed about 150 pounds, but when he stood up to preach, he would seem about ten feet tall. He was a good preacher. I admired and respected him highly because this man lived the life that he preached about. He would visit the sick in the hospital and fulfill all other duties of a church leader.

I remember when Rodney, my baby son, was coming home from school one day, and he was hit by a car. The accident was reported on the police scanner and radio. Somehow, Rev. Beacoat heard about it and was at the hospital before the ambulance could get there. I was getting off work, and when I got home, I got the call to go to the hospital right away. My wife was going to work and saw the crowd standing over someone. She noticed that the coat on the ground was our son's so she pulled over and broke through the crowd, and there lay Rodney. She began to scream and cry, and my son looked up at her and said, "Don't cry, Momma I'm okay." She told me later that when she got to the hospital, Rev. Beacoat was there. He said that he did not want to get in anyone's way, but he was there to pray for us. Yes, that man was a good person, and he lived the life he preached about. Thank God Rodney was okay and grew up to be an outstanding young man whom I am very proud of. The doctor who took care of him decided that he would keep Rodney overnight.

The job at Ziegler was a blessing. The factory produced heaters and air-conditioners. The factory had three shifts; I worked in the mornings, and Novella worked in the evenings. That way, there would always be someone home with our children. Novella started working there after she left her job at the hospital. She enjoyed working in the medical field, but Ziegler paid higher wages. With the income we made, we were able to pay our bills that we left in Hammond and our bills we accumulated in Centralia. The wages we made in the North were higher than the wages we earned in the South. We were renting from TB but decided that we needed our own home, so we went to our credit union to see if we could get a loan to purchase a house.

The beautiful thing about the company we worked for was that they allowed their employees to buy shares in the company, and then we could borrow money from our shares. So when Novella and I decided that it was time to purchase our own home, we went to the company and got the money. The search for a place to live in was not as simple as I thought it would be. In this small town, it was all about whether or not they knew you or your family. Finally, the pastor found out that we were looking for a place to live and offered his mother's old house with the option to rent before buying. We went to look at the area, and we really liked the house on Locust Street. I remember driving down the tree-lined street and thinking how warm and inviting the neighborhood seemed to be. We moved in to the house and really liked living there, but another house came up for sale on the same street, and we wanted to buy it because it the lot was very big. So we went back to our credit union to get more money, but this time the credit union refused to give us the money. So we both went in and explained that we wanted the house because of the land, and the house was bigger than the house we were living in. The manager of the credit union listened to our plans to rent out the house we bought from Rev. Beacoat, and the extra money could be used to pay back the loan. The loan was approved, and we purchased our second home within two years of moving up north. God is good. The new house also had only two bedrooms, so we had to add rooms to the house. It was interesting how Novella got the man to reconsider giving us the loan. I did realize what a great head she had for business. At our new home, we added a bedroom, bath, and family room, and expanded the kitchen and added on a two-car garage. We had the biggest lot on the street. This was a very good place to raise children.

On Sunday mornings, we would go to Sunday school and church service. When we came home from church, we would play games or sleep. In the summer months, the children would go swimming. It was a simple life style, but we enjoyed one another as a family. It was all we knew up north because the larger part of the family was down south. Novella and I would make vacation plans to visit the South where our family lived. This would ensure that the children would stay connected to their family roots and that the family would stay familiar with them.

Every year, my family and I would travel from Centralia to Louisiana. That was the big event of the year. The trip was seven hundred miles one way. We always traveled at night, so the children would sleep through a lot of the trip. We all looked forward to our summer vacation, and there were so many stories and great memories surrounding those trips; to tell them all, it would take more than one book. I thank God for those memories, and I know that my children do also because I hear them talk about those trips often.

CHAPTER FOURTEEN

My Job as a Welder

On my new job, I was assigned to the welding department although I had never worked as a welder before. The position provided training. The company was very big in helping their employees learn their trade well. The company provided education for those who wanted to move up in the company to higher salaries. The class taught different techniques to weld, so I went to school to improve my job skills. I became the third welder at the company. I wanted to improve my position at the company, and education was the way to move forward. The welding department had about forty employees. The whole plant had five hundred. The company itself was large; it had factories in twelve states and a factory in Japan. Ziegler was a large company, and the workers were proud to work for a company that allowed them to have a share in the company. Another plus was that the company offered all the overtime that we wanted, and it never seemed to wear out. Novella decided to leave the medical field and join me at the factory. She worked in a different department, but it was nice to know that she was close. We decided to work different shifts because we wanted one of us to be home when the children came home from school. I worked the morning shift, and my wife worked the second shift from three to eleven. We would see each other when we clocked in and out at the time clock.

I soon learned that being at home with the children was a job in itself. I had to take my daughter to basketball games because she was a cheerleader, and my sons had Boy Scout meetings and sporting events to attend. I also had church in the evening. I always took my children to prayer meetings and choir rehearsal. I was very busy, but I always enjoyed the extra activities. I remember one school activity where the parents were asked to bring a covered dish to a school function. The children told me that parents were asked to bring a covered dish to the school's activity. The children and I got ready for the school function, I got my covered dish, and we headed out for the school. There was a long line of individuals dropping off their dish, and we got into the line to drop our dish off.

Our neighbor was the person collecting the dish, and she was one of my favorite people because she loved to talk and had a great sense of humor. When I got to her, she asked, "Brother Walls, did you bring your covered dish?" I proudly displayed one of my wife's beautiful casserole dishes and proceeded to take the cover off to show her my dish. She looked inside, and a big smile came on her face that quickly turned into a full blown laughter. She tried to hide it by turning her back to me and placing her hand over her mouth. I realized then that something was supposed to be in the dish; I later learned from my wife that that something was *food*. It could have been green beans, carrots, casserole etc. I went and sat down because all I could see were my friend's shoulder moving hysterically up and down. The children and I took our seats, and I knew I would have to hear about this later, the first time my neighbor ran into my wife. I decided to enjoy the evening and one day include the fiasco in my book. As I suspected, my wife ran into her, and she told her what happened. They both laughed about it, but my wife forbade me from going to school functions unless she made sure that everything was in place on our part.

I was also my boys' scout leader, and we were required to meet once a week. The boys were in the age range of eight to eleven. My daughter had to come with us, and she was the only girl at the meeting, but she made the adjustments just as we all did for the family.

The role of my being home with the children at night was about to change. After five years of working at the company, the employees voted to have a union, the teamster union. A lot of changes happened I was chosen to be the steward for the union. If anything went wrong in the company, the union had the right to strike. I was the in-between person taking information to the supervisors from the employees and delivering the response back to the workers.

The union was good and bad for the company. The bad news came when we learned that we could not have shares in the company. The union stated that if we had stock in the company and were part-owners, the union would be of no use to us. The union brought us some security, but we were no longer part-owners of the company.

Although there were changes going on with the company, I still considered the job steady work. We could always plan for our vacations to be taken around the same time. I enjoyed the annual trip to Louisiana to visit family and friends. I really enjoyed those wonderful vacation checks that my wife and I accumulated. I remember going to the bank cashing a twelve-hundred-dollar check just for our trip. I did not want those checks to ever stop, but all good things must come to an end. But when they do, God has another door for you to go through and enjoy even more blessings.

The company started to have layoffs, and they started closing their companies in other states. My wife and I discussed this as we were traveling to Louisiana one year. We were entering Memphis and used that as a marker to determine how much longer the trip was going to take. We knew when we would get to Memphis that we were halfway through our trip. My wife and I would discuss everything along the way, and we decided that if the plant closed down, God would open a window of opportunity for us. Novella and I were and still are very optimistic people. I remember stopping at the rest stop in Memphis and allowing the children to eat and afterward run off their pent-up energy. Yes, I enjoyed those trips so much. We had a lot of strange events happen to us on our trips to and from the North and South.

I remember one time we were on the road, about ten years after we relocated, we were going down south to my mother-in-law's funeral. We were driving our minivan. Now my wife would always warn me about making sure we had enough gas because the van did not have a large reserve. I really don't understand why, but I liked to push cars. I would try and use every drop of gas possible before I refilled. It was an internal game between my car and me. My wife hated it, and she was always warning me about the gas gauge in the car. I reassured her that I knew exactly how far the car would go and the amount of gas that I needed to get it there. Well, as we entered the state of Mississippi, I had decided to find a station to stop at and refill, but my intentions were interrupted by a sudden exhausted sound from the engine. Yes, my van had run out of gas and gave a resounding last gasp, as if seeking oxygen, and stopped as I used the little energy left to pull onto the side of the interstate. I dared not look at my beautiful but furious wife sitting next to me, so I just announced to the air and to anyone listening that I was going to walk to the nearest gas station.

I proceeded to the back of the van and found the gas can under the pile of luggage and started out on my journey. As I got about a half mile from the van, a very nice car pulled up next to me. The driver in the car was a well-groomed Caucasian man, and his wife and children were also in the car. The man asked me if I would like a ride, and I replied yes I would. As we traveled down the interstate in search of a gas station, he told me that he saw my wife and daughter in my van on the side of the road. He also told me that he was a preacher and was headed to some city in Mississippi to run a revival. The conversation was nice, and we finally found a gas station about five miles down the road.

He drove me back to my car, and I asked him, "How much do I owe you?"

He said, "Nothing."

I held a five-dollar bill in my hand and tried to give it to him, but he would not take it, He told me to use that money to help someone in need. I said thank-you, and we put the gas in the car and started back on our journey. Novella was still a little angry with me, but she slowly let go of her anger, which is one of the qualities I love about her. She doesn't nag or complain about things; she forgives easily. After traveling about eighty miles down the highway, we decided to stop at a rest area to stretch and use the restroom. At the rest area, there was a woman and her son sitting on the bench in front of the station. As I passed by, she asked me for gas money to help her get to Texas. She said that she was nearly out of gas and needed money for gas. I said "of course" and gave her two dollars.

When my wife came from the restroom, I told her the story, and she said, "Why didn't you give her the five dollars the man told you to use in helping someone?" I did not know what to say because I had no valid reason. She went to the woman and gave her three more dollars.

Another time when we headed to Louisiana for a visit, we had a mishap. It was Novella and I along with two of our children, my youngest son, Eric, and my youngest daughter, Crystal. The trip, as usual, included the stern warning from my dear wife about keeping the tank full. I appeased her the entire trip by making sure the tank was full, but on the last stretch, I decided that my car had to be tested again to determine how far she would go. I, of course, did not share my plan with my beautiful wife. So we made it into the state of Louisiana, we were about twenty-five miles from our destination, and guess what happened? Yes, we ran out of gas. It was early in the morning, around four o'clock, when everyone, even in the south, was well into a good sleep. Surprisingly, my wife was quiet about our predicament. I looked over at her, and she had a look of concern that was so different from her mad look. I saw her looking around as if she expected something to happen, and that is when it dawned on me where we were. We had ran out of gas in an all-white town, one we were familiar with from our childhood—a town that used to not allow black people to live in it safely—and that is when I knew we were again in the South.

I told Novella that I was walking to the nearest gas station for help. She looked at me as if she wanted to say something, but she kept quiet. The children were asleep in the back, not conscious of what was going on in our world. As I was walking, I spotted a pay phone not even two blocks from where I left Novella and the children, which was a big blessing. I did not want to leave them alone for a significant amount of time in this area. I called my brother and told him what had happened and where we were. In fifteen minutes, he was there with gas and a big smile. He teasingly gave my wife twenty dollars and said, "Girl, don't let that boy run out of gas with you and the children in the car."

So after we agreed to meet and talk later on, he left, and we continued on to my mother-in-law's house. There is something so endearing about other in-laws, especially mine. She was the only one I ever had, and she was the best. I liked going to her house because she always had my favorite foods waiting for me to eat. She would tell her other daughters, "Fix Lee a plate of butter beans and okra." She knew that was my favorite meal, and she always had it there waiting for me. I miss her so much. Others complain about their mother-in-law. I never did because she was so sweet and nice. I can't say the same about others in the family, especially when they were annoyed because we did not make it to their houses when we visited. We would say to them, "We have traveled seven hundred miles. Can't you come the ten miles to see us?" We still went to them a lot of the times because that was how we were, and we always had a lot of fun when we did give in and go visit other family-members, even if they lived in another state.

CHAPTER FIFTEEN

Hammond Revisited

We were amazed at how much Hammond had grown. The population had more than doubled since we moved up north. We realized that there would be change, but the changes were very significant even with the change in people. We left in the late sixties when the population was ten thousand people, and now, in the eighties, there were sixty thousand people. There were highways and interstates running through the town, and business popped up all over the place.

I was raised in Hammond, and everyone knew one another's families, but I did not recognize people nor did I know their families. This surprised me because I never thought that would be possible. I recall being at a store with my wife when two young men walked over to us, one leading the other. They seemed to be in their middle twenties. The one who was smiling and leading the other by the shoulder asked him, "Do you know who this man is?" The other replied that he did not recognize me, which I felt was fitting because I did not recognize either of them. To my delight and surprise, the guy with the big smile said, "This is our Sunday-school teacher when we were kids." We all laughed and caught up on what was going on in our lives. I used to teach a class of students from the ages of eight to sixteen, and it was such a blessing to know that they still remembered me in such a favorable way.

After I returned back to Illinois from Louisiana, I was ready to go back to work. I enjoyed my two weeks' vacation, but I also enjoyed working. I believe it is because I was a sharecropper's son and working was an integral part of my life. My father taught me that work is what you make out of it; you can make it fun or miserable—it's up to your mind-set.

The next day, I received a call from my bank. The teller said, "Hello, is this Leroy Walls?"

I said, "Yes."

The teller said, "Our records show that you were in the bank two weeks ago, cashed a check, and the teller gave you a hundred dollars more than she should. Did you receive the extra money?"

I told her that I did receive the money and that we were headed for Louisiana after the transaction, so we were not turning around to come back and straighten out the mishap.

The teller got quiet and then put on her polite voice again and asked, "Will you return the money to the bank?"

I said to her, "I have been on vacation, and I spent the money."

Again there was silence, and then she asked, "Would you pay the money back on a monthly plan?"

I told her yes, I would, so we agreed to open an account at that bank, and I would pay twenty-five dollars a pay period until I paid the money back. Novella and I found the whole incident strange because we tried to open an account at that bank, and they would not allow us to because they said we had not been in the area long enough. But because this happened, they allowed us to open an account, and we had the account for our entire stay in Centralia. The blessing was that after we paid off the one hundred dollars, we could go and get a loan anytime we needed to. Another blessing was how the employees treated us; they were very friendly and nice to Novella and me, and we made a lot of friends that would invite us to their homes. Some of them had large farms that they would invite Novella and I to come and visit. We met some interesting people.

I remember one guy I met who was frugal. He would not spend a dime if he had to. I often joked with him about squeezing a dollar so tight. His wife wanted a shed to be built in the back of her yard, and he decided that he would build it rather than spend a lot of money hiring a professional. After he constructed the building, I went out to look at his handiwork. The shed did not look sturdy, but I wasn't about to tell him of my true opinion of his handiwork. His wife was not as kind. She consistently pointed out all the imperfections and how cheap he was for not hiring a professional to do the work. My wife and I were getting uncomfortable with the arguing between the two and vowed not to get involved with our opinions. The next day, the wife got on her tractor and hitched the shed up to it to pull the shed out into the middle of the field. She said that it was a pile of junk, and she did not want it near her house.

Another acquaintance I met was a nice man in his midforties. He had a rural, rugged look about him. As a matter of fact, if you saw him, you would assume that he had the textbook appearance of someone who was a hardcore farmer, someone who would not be interested in or tolerable of other cultures, but that was not the case. He and I were good friends. It did not matter what color a person's skin was, I respected them as long as the respect was mutual. I enjoyed his company, and we had some great conversations. I recall once talking about family, and he shared with me about a family dispute between him and his brother. He had not spoken to his brother for fifteen years over a fight they had about a gas can. At the time, I found this to be one of the most unbelievable stories ever. How could brothers not speak to each other for fifteen years and live in the same area? How could a family be so divided by something as jejune as a gas can? I talked to him about the Bible and what the Bible said about forgiveness, and he did listen.

There was another couple we met who had been married for a long time, and the wife was going blind. The husband was really sad about his wife's condition; we used to talk for long periods of time about her condition. The husband decided to give the wife one of his eyes because he loved her that much. I really respected this man because in my mind, that is what you call real love. The doctors operated on them, and it was a success. The eye worked just fine in the wife's body, and now she could see. This story should have had a happy ending, but it did not. After one more year of marriage, she ran off with another man, taking his eye with her.

On the job, we had a lot of married couples working together like Novella and me. One couple was always in a fight and one threatened to leave the other. Well, one day after work, he went home to find that the trailer was gone. She hauled off the trailer with everything in it and left him nothing. We listened to him call her all sorts of names using choice words to describe everything about her existence. Novella and I used to say, "There is never a dull moment in this workplace or town. There is always something going on."

One story line was not so funny. The fact that the factory was really closing meant that my wife and I were both out of work. We had huge savings, but if we did not find work, that would dwindle down and eventually be exhausted. We had four children by now; our youngest son, Eric, was born, the only one of our children to be born up north. Well,

Novella and I decided to put all our trust in God. Novella said to me as we were driving one day after we heard the news, "What are we going to do, Lee? Our family is seven hundred miles away, and both of us are out of work."

I said to her, "My Father is rich, and he owns cattle on a thousand hills, and he owns everything. He will take care of us." At first she pondered over what I was saying knowing my father had been dead for years, then a smile took over her once-concerned-looking appearance, and she said in agreement with me, "Yes, our Father in heaven will provide."

CHAPTER SIXTEEN

Correction Officer

One day while we were going through our daily mail, we came across a letter with the state seal on it. We believed it was a letter telling us that our older son and daughter had accumulated more traffic tickets, something that the both of them were becoming notorious for doing. It seemed that every time I turned around, they were getting tickets, so I put it to the side and opened the rest of the mail. Forgetting the letter, I went to work on chores around the house. I decided that I would catch up with much-needed work around the house while I was off work. I began to repair and build any and all parts of the house. While getting all the trash together to start my burn pile, the letter with the state seal was on top of all that trash, sticking out like a sore thumb. The envelope had a virginal appearance, white without a stain, wrinkle, or crease on the envelope, and the seal was still intact because no one had opened it. I gave the "being responsible" sigh and grabbed the piece of mail to open it and get the much-dreaded news. The letter was, to my surprise, not a letter stating that my children were getting more traffic tickets. The letter was offering me the opportunity to work for the state of Illinois.

I was very excited about the offer to have another employer but was very curious about the facility. The letter stated that it was corrections, and the only correction facility I knew about was the one in Louisiana called Angola Prison. The place was a very bad facility to be at or work at. I believe that the workers were required to live at the facility on weekends. I wondered if the state of Illinois used those same rules and regulations, so I called the number on the letter, and they asked me to come in for an interview. They gave me instructions on how to get to the facility in a place called Vandalia, Illinois. Vandalia was about thirty miles away from Centralia, and to my surprise, the town was smaller than Centralia. The population of African Americans in the town was small—I believe about 1 percent black, if that much. I did not concern myself with that bit of information because I was from the South and had experienced all sorts of diversity, and it prepared me for the North.

The next week, I went to the correctional facility for an interview. When I arrived at the facility, there were guards who checked my credentials to make sure I belonged there. After that, I walked through the gate and saw a lot of young men there who were exercising and playing games on the grounds. I walked past them to a building with several offices and guards standing nearby. I was seated and told that the interview would begin shortly. While sitting there, I thought about God and how great he was, getting me the job before I was through with my old job. A man came to the door and told me that I could come in at this time.

Walking through the door, I felt assured and confident. There were three men sitting at a table. As I sat down, I knew that the position was mine. The men asked me if I would like to work here at the correctional facility. I told them that I would like to have a job because my old job was closing and that I had a family that I needed to support. They seemed to like my response and asked if I had any questions. I did. I asked them about the weapon I would be using to guard the inmates. They all looked at each other with a look of surprise and said, "The correctional officers don't carry guns."

I then looked surprise and asked, "How do we control them?"

They said that "we control them with pen and paper."

I was more than a little surprised because the concept of controlling all those big guys with a piece of paper and a pen intrigued me. The one observation that I made as I was passing through the prison yards was how physically powerful their presence was. I just assumed that the officers had a gun that they used for protection. They assured me that the inmates fought each other and very seldom attacked an officer, so the officers did not need a gun. The interview crew assured me that I would receive all the training that I would need in working with the prisoners. They offered me the job with a salary that I was very pleased with. Although all sounded well, I explained to them that I could not take the job for two weeks. I had committed myself to my old employer to help close the factory down.

They had offered me an extra two hundred dollars to come back and help with the final shutdown. They said okay and gave me three new uniforms and a cap. I was glad to have a new job—and a job that paid me a lot more than I was making at Ziegler's. God is good! I went home and told my wife about everything that happened, and she was happy too.

CHAPTER SEVENTEEN

Corrections

We were sent to Chicago to attend the police academy for sixteen weeks of training. On the way to the facility, I remember seeing a sign that read "We are the peoples, none of us is smarter than all of us." At the college, there were different kinds of men that had different ideas that they brought to the table. The instructors took pride in the academy. They reminded us that after we graduated, we would be representatives of the academy, so we should watch how we conducted ourselves. They also told us that none of us are above the law, so we should be very careful. Those words went into my psyche. I never broke the law because I am a Christian, but there words stayed with me throughout my career as an officer and then later as a sergeant.

At the academy, there were numerous buildings that housed other trainees in law enforcement. At night, the officers would go to different bars in the city or other places that I was not accustomed to going. They would go in groups because a large part of our training stressed the importance of going together in groups rather than by ourselves, especially in a large city such as Chicago. They shared with us that a lot of people in the city did not like police officers or anyone who represented the law. I decided that I would use my free time by going to the park. What harm could happen to you at the park? The park was only a three-block walk at the most. Even though I was alone (because I didn't frequent bars or do the things the other officers were doing), I felt I would be safe.

I loved the fact that the academy was not located far from the park because the more stressful a situation was, the more relaxation time one should have; not just a "chemical stimulation" type of relaxation but a "day in the park with nature" type of relaxation. One day while I was walking to the park, still in my uniform, I began thinking about Novella and the children when a truck drove by with a few men on the back of it. These men started yelling "Hi ho, black boy!" over and over. I was surprised because this was the north, and I did not know people rode on the back of trucks here. That experience taught me two things: never walk alone and never wear my uniform if I am alone. Other than that incident, I really enjoyed the academy.

The academy brought to my attention how important training was when using a weapon. Being raised in the South, having a weapon was part of life. No one had training, but everyone had a rifle to hunt with for food. They provided a lot of training on how you should never play with a gun. I found that odd because I never knew people who would actually play with a gun, but the academy spent a lot of time explaining why that was absolutely unacceptable. We learned what weapons to use in the case of ever being attacked; the academy taught me that not all weapons were the same. We learned about weapons to use in case an inmate attacked us. The most important weapon I learned about was the weapon above my shoulders; they taught us that the head was the best weapon to use in any stressful or potentially deadly attack.

They stressed the importance of being fair in all situations; we were always supposed to represent the law. Whenever the inmates tried to challenge us, we were to always remind them that we represented the law and that we were to abide by the law just like them. This type of talking always gave the inmates the sense that everyone was on the same page, and everyone was treated the same. I used that information throughout my career in corrections. I always reminded the inmates that I did not make the rules but was being paid to enforce them. The majority of the time, they accepted that explanation, and I never really had to use any other type of weapon other than my head.

The biggest revelation for me was when I discovered that so many people did not like people who worked for the law. I always respected the policemen and others in law enforcement. I was surprised when we would travel to other places in the city and be treated with resentment. When we wore our uniforms, we were often denied the use of their phones at certain service stations, and the looks we would get were not pleasant. This was not the story all the time, but I was surprised at the times we did get this type of treatment. At the academy, we were taught that we were to help people in need. That was the motto to help and serve the public.

After being at the academy for sixteen weeks, we had a graduation. Afterward, we took pictures, and we all said our good-byes. The one thing that stuck out for me was the code, which was "we the people" and "none of us are smarter than all of us, so stay strong and stick together." On your life journey, remember that whatever you do, someone can see you when you least expect it, so do the right thing. I loved this way of thinking because it is Christian; it is what the army also taught.

In the army, we were taught that when we put our uniforms on, we were representing the United States of America. The uniform is a representation of something bigger than us. I had training in Chicago, Illinois, and training in Springfield, Illinois, and both trainings gave me a college credit, so I was very proud of my training. I was praying that it really would prepare me for my work in corrections.

The training at the academy in Springfield should prepare anyone. The training was vigorous and more physical than mental. I recall in one of my trainings that the officers had the sticks they used when pursuing a criminal, and they would provide you with one too. They would swing the stick at you and hit you if you did not defend yourself. So I was surprised at the aggressiveness of the officers. I learned a lot at the academy. There were different types of gases that could be used to hold off inmates if they got out of hand. One gas could make you laugh while another would bring tears to your eyes. The most potent gas would make you pass out wherever you were standing. The gas that I found to be the most interesting was the gas that could make you feel as if you were choking. The most dangerous gas of all was the one you could neither see nor smell.

At the academy, we learned to work with one another and look out for one another. I remembered the sign that I read coming into the academy and understood the meaning behind the words. The words to me made sense, and I decided that I would keep the words fresh in my mind, especially when I went to work in the correctional facility. I learned that in a group, we were only as strong as the weakest group member. The academy taught us to not trust the population so quickly because they were inmates because you can't let the inmates get anything by you. We learned about the four types of people we would be working with. They were identifies as the good, bad, ugly, and the other. I understood what they were saying to us, to just be careful, and we should be able to depend on our fellow officers for any support needed.

After the training was over, we had a party and took pictures celebrating our accomplishment and the return home. This time spent away from home reminded me of when I was stationed in Fort Hood, Texas, training to go to Korea for the army. It brought me into contact with all types of people, and the lesson was always that we had to work together. The lessons I learned from both was that we all have to trust God and stick together as humans, that the color of our skin is secondary when we are faced with danger; the neighborhood we come from is different when we face danger. The biggest and most prevalent instinct is to stick together and survive the threat.

At the Correctional Center / Behind the Bars

After returning from the academy, I was placed in Vandalia's correctional facility. I lived approximately thirty miles away, but the ride was never an issue for me. I enjoyed the time alone to pray and go over my concerns of the day. Although I enjoyed the privacy and alone-time with God, I found it cost-effective if I carpooled with other officers. There was also a sense of comradery because we talked about the job and about issues, inmates, and other concerns regarding the facility.

The other officers at Vandalia seemed happy to have new officers. The commander assigned each officer to a dorm that they would be responsible for the operation and function of. The dorms were labeled using the letters of the alphabet. Each dorm housed anywhere from eighty to one hundred inmates. There was one assigned officer to the dorms. The duties of the officers were to keep count of all the inmates, to pass out meds, and to pass out mail. The inmates were always happy if they received mail that was uplifting. If any of you have someone you know that is incarcerated, please write them a letter of encouragement. It means a lot to someone who is locked up and cut off from family and friends.

The job was not as stressful as I thought it might be. When I first heard about corrections, I felt that the hardest part of the job was trying to stay safe. I soon realized that I really was not in immediate danger twenty-four hours a day. I understood why the academy stressed how important it was for us to work together as a team. When you go into the facility and have the mind-set of team, there really is no big danger. Of course there were fights, but the inmates almost always fought against each other. It was rare and seldom that an inmate would hit an officer. When there were fights in the facility, there was always backup at the scene within two minutes. Inmates respected the officers because they knew that the officers held a lot of power in their pens and their paper tickets.

My first dorm was *L* dorm; my inmates would be assigned to a job or a school class. The inmates were encouraged to keep busy, and the facility provided numerous jobs on the grounds. A lot of inmates did kitchen work; the work allowed them access to the kitchen and the food. The inmates cooked and maintained all functions of the smoothly running kitchen. I liked the idea of the inmates working; it gave them something to do so the time would pass by sooner. Everyone was allowed to eat during his or her eight-hour shift. I remember going through the line and hearing one of the inmates give me a warning to not eat a certain dish. I always heeded their advice because I knew they had access to the food, and because of this knowledge, I always prayed and gave thanks at every meal eaten at the facility. I asked God to bless the food. There were other jobs that the inmates did. For instance, they worked on the farm milking cows and cutting the lawn. The facility had acreage of land that the inmates would keep in tip-top shape.

The inmates were also given the opportunity to get their diplomas and degrees for school. They would work very hard on their courses in school, hoping to be able to get a job upon their release. I respected the inmates who were really trying to turn their lives around. They had decided that incarceration was not for them. I got the chance to talk one-on-one with a lot of the inmates. I enjoyed the conversations and had my clearest understanding of respecting others and they will respect you.

Sunday was my biggest day to talk with individuals one-on-one. Sunday was a day of rest just like on the outside. The inmates had chapel, and it was open to everyone. The chapel could hold about three hundred people but only thirty or forty inmates would attend. The inmates would stay in to watch television or to strike up a card game. I used this time to seek out inmates and talk with them about their plans for the future or about my Lord and Savior Jesus Christ.

The one observation that surprised me was the percentage of black inmates. The facility held approximately 750 inmates, and 90 percent was minority. The majority population on the outside did not reflect the majority population that was locked up. I was amazed because throughout my career in corrections, I had the chance to visit many correctional facilities in the state, and at each facility, the largest population of inmates was the minority. This bothered me because I was seeing these numbers, and something wasn't adding up.

I remember my first experience of a riot at the prison. It was in the seventies, and it was over a television show called *Roots* based on the novel by Alex Haley. The inmates were all watching the show and had strong opinions about the program. The black inmates started complaining about the treatment of the slaves and were calling out derogatory names and remarks; the white inmates did not like the names and language being used. In my dorm, I had about seventy inmates. Forty of the inmates were black and thirty were white, so I was really concerned. The blacks were projecting their anger toward the white inmates, and it was beginning to get serious. The state sent in buses to transport prisoners to other facilities until things cooled down. I got to see firsthand how a riot was handled at the facility. From this experience, I also learned that when a safety issue was at stake, it didn't matter what color you are nor too much of anything else; what did matter in this type of situation was what uniform you have on, and that is it, point blank. The experience confirmed my beliefs in doing the right thing. It didn't matter who liked or disliked me. Race did not matter. The only thing that was my biggest concern was to do what I was taught to do with integrity and without prejudice, and that's what I did.

I remember when I started as a lieutenant. There was a group of officers called the tactical unit. This team was used if there was any type of disturbance in the facility that required order in a way harsher than just the regular way of maintaining order. These units had men in charge that often gave us sound advice when it came to maintaining control in the facility. There was this lieutenant who did not follow the same lead; he was a man who seemed a little bitter toward his job and really should have retired years ago. He took me to the side after training one day and suggested to me that if I ever had an unruly inmate who would not conform, there were ways to get him out of the institution and, therefore, out of my hair. I eagerly listened because I wanted the sound advice, but what he told me was illegal, and I refused to even indulge in the conversation any longer.

There are negative people in all occupations, but the good ones are larger in numbers in the correction field. I always went by the rules; I could not do it any other way. Following the rules made my job easier because if an inmate would ask me, "Why are you forcing us to do it this way?" I would always say, "Because those are the rules." I also would add that I didn't make the rules, I just enforced them. Also, when I wrote an inmate a ticket for breaking a rule, I made sure they knew what rule they had broken before I would write the ticket.

I remember a very bad accident that happened on the job. I had been a t the facility for about six months, and we were out on the range practicing using weapons. We were about ten miles from the correction center when we spotted a bus that had stopped. The bus had a full load of inmates, so I'm guessing around fifty or so. The rules were that all the inmates had to be locked together and were held together by a chain that was attached to all the prisoners. This, of course, was for safety precautions so none of the inmates would escape from custody. This was the normal procedure when transporting inmates by bus or van. There was usually more than one officer that would escort a busload of inmates, but only one of the escorts would have the key to unlock the inmates.

While waiting, one of the inmates decided to smoke, but while he was lighting his cigarette, the lit match fell and started a fire on the bus. There was a lot of confusion on the bus. The inmates were yelling and swearing at us to unlock them and let them out of the burning bus. The problem was that the person who had the one key to unlock the inmates' chain had left to try and get help for the stopped bus. We did not know what to do because it would have been too difficult within that time frame to break chains and doors. The flames were rising, the bus was getting hotter, and the inmates were yelling profusely. So someone from our bus found an ax that was with our supplies. He climbed on top of the bus and tried to free the men by cutting away the top of the bus. His efforts were admirable, but it all turned out to be a tragic episode; while the officer was chopping into the bus with his ax, he hit an inmate in the top of his head and killed him. The officer with the key returned moments after the accident, and we were able to get on the smoke-engulfed bus to help the surviving inmates. That was a very bad accident, one that I will always remember as a good gesture having bad results.

Working at a correctional center, you must always be on guard for anything that could happen, and hope and pray that nothing bad happens. We had to search the inmates daily, especially when they went out on the yard. We were always looking for weapons that might be used to injure another inmate or an officer because when they all gathered out on the yard, it was a large crowd; and if someone wanted to get revenge or just hurt someone, that would be the opportunity to do so. So we searched them thoroughly before allowing them to go outside.

The routine usually was that the lieutenant would group them, and the officers would go in their rooms and look for weapons and search them for weapons. I was "shaking down" an inmate, which is another term for searching them, and I discovered a knife hidden in his bed. The knife was about a foot long and very sharp. I retrieved the knife and took it to the lieutenant. From that day on, I double-searched the inmates and their rooms. I never took my position lightly at the prison because taking it lightly could be a matter of life or death.

Another surprise for me was the number of people who did not like you because, as a correctional officer, it meant you were "watching" some of their loved ones. They blamed you for their loved ones being locked up behind bars. I remember when we used to take trips for training and how we were not allowed to use the restrooms at some service stations. I remember having the bus stop and walking to people's homes, and they refused to let us use their phones to call for help, but we were always willing to help others in distress. When we would see a car pulled on the side of the road, if we could, we would stop and help.

One time, there was a bad car accident, and we stopped and helped direct traffic until the police officers arrived. Witnessing how much the public in my area did not want to help out officers, my wife and I decided to have codes to alert each other when we were in need of help. We also taught our children codes to use if they were in trouble and needed assistance.

One night while traveling home, my car stopped. It was very late at night, and it was literally freezing outside. Temperatures were so low that there were advisories throughout the Midwest warning people to not venture outside unless they had an emergency. I was stranded about twenty miles from my home, so I was a little concerned but not a lot. I knew that God had my situation in his hands, and all would be well. After about a five-minute wait, an eighteen-wheeler pulled in behind me and asked if I needed help. I told him yes. I gave him my phone number and asked him to stop at a phone to give my wife this message, "The rabbit is in trouble on Highway 51."

He looked at me and smiled. He said, "Okay, I will call this number and relay the message."

When my wife got the message, she understood every word spoken. She immediately woke up my son and said, "Go out there and help your father. He has car trouble on the highway." In about thirty minutes, my son Rodney pulled up, and I was so happy to see him.

There were a lot of strange things happening on the road at night, so I was happy to have a way to communicate to my family when I was in trouble. I did not worry about all those strange happenings because I knew God would take care of me, and he did. I remember there was snow everywhere, but I pushed through. The lane had transformed into a one-lane highway because the snow was too thick for the road to be divided any farther. I could barely see what was in front of me, but I could not turn back because the traffic was bumper-to-bumper. When I arrived at work, I discovered that most of the staff was stuck at home. Although a lot of the employees lived closer to the institution than I did, it seemed that a lot of them got stuck in their driveways at their houses. The ones who got to work had to pull double shifts, which was not good when you worked at a place where you had to be mentally alert.

Another incident occurred one night after work. My car pooler and I were traveling home when this lady in only a slip popped up out of nowhere. She had no other clothes on nor did she have shoes on. We looked at each other, questioning whether or not to stop as she was flagging us down and begging for us to stop. We stopped, and she said her husband was after her to beat her up. We called for help, and the police soon arrived. The police were sometimes friendly, but other times, they could be difficult. I remember one policeman telling us that we were the law on the inside of the prison, but on the outside, they were the law and that we should know our place. I always felt that we were on the same side, the side of the law. They had the job of arresting; we had the job of correcting.

Some might not realize how often a correctional officer is placed in dangerous positions. For instance, we had to transport prisoners to court, funerals, and anywhere else they might need to be. Yes, we would have weapons, but we did not have backup as the policemen did. Once, when an officer took an inmate to his mother's funeral, there were relatives waiting there who shot up the place trying to get the inmate out the backdoor to freedom. His plan did not succeed because other relatives helped the correctional officers out.

There were usually two officers to one inmate when we traveled with them. I remember taking inmates to funerals and there would be family who tried to intimidate us by walking close behind us or staring at us with threatening glares. I was glad to have the gun because there were moments when I felt as though I might need it. I am glad that I never did use my weapon, but it helped us feel safe.

I was glad when we changed the way the inmate viewed the deceased. It used to be that they attended when the family did, but it was changed to where the inmate could only view before the funeral or after. This way ensured that the officer was safer by not being in a hostile environment and the inmate was not approached by someone who would be rude to him. I remember when I attended a funeral session with a pretty decent inmate. When he went to view the body, his sister ran up to him and started yelling and screaming at him. He responded to her aggressiveness with aggression, so we had to get him out of there fast. It was always different in every situation.

When we transported inmates, we had a specific time to check back in just in case something went wrong. There have been stories of inmates having gang members or old girlfriends meet us on the road trying to get us to pull over so they could help the inmate to escape, so we never stopped on the road when we had an inmate in our care. We sometimes had a hard time calling back because this was the era before cell phone popularity, so we used pay phones. If we were passing another correctional facility, we would call back and check in with our location and time.

There were only two places that refused to let us use their phones, and surprisingly enough, it was another state facility that housed juvenile inmates. The second place was a gas station with an attendant who looked as if she was angry at the world. Looking at us from head to toe in our creased, sharp, and shining uniforms, she snarled at us, "No!"

I really did not understand people not helping each other. Being a Christian, I always felt that helping people was God's plan for us all. Imagine how Jesus would feel if we did not have it in our hearts to help people in need, especially when Jesus died for our sins, and especially when his ministry was always showing how righteous it is to help others. Remember how he fed the people who came out to hear his words, and it got late in the evening; how he had compassion for them and blessed the number of fish so that the disciples were able to feed them all and have some left over. Jesus performed miracles daily. He helped so many people who were ill and needed a miracle.

I remember one time being in Sunday school and hearing a speech from a woman minister. She was speaking about how we as Christians should show love and kindness to all, especially to people who are not saved. This speaker was saying that we should model Christ as much as is needed because people were looking at us to always do the right thing. The words that stuck in my mind were, "If they knew better, they would do better."

So many times, Christians are judged and condemned without the benefit of being heard. If a person who is not a Christian got upset and raised their voice, it is considered normal; but if a person who is called a Christian would do the same thing, their entire walk with God is questioned. Therefore, as Christians, we have to keep Jesus in our hearts and minds constantly, understanding that we are the representatives of what the church is supposed to look like. The Bible teaches us that if Christ is in you, your body is dead because of sin, yet your spirit is alive because of righteousness (Romans 8:10). It goes on to say that if the spirit of he who raised Jesus from the dead is living in you, he who raised Christ from the dead will also give you life to your mortal body through his spirit who lives in you. We are the righteousness of God; God's spirit lives in us.

I always carried God in my heart even when I was in Korea. There were times when I just could not go along with what the other soldiers were doing, and how mean some were to the people who lived in the area. On one assignment, we were instructed to go to a specific area and practice using our weapons. We were to make sure that all the civilians were out of the area before we started shooting. Now some of the Koreans were older ones, and they obviously moved slowly. Some of the men in my unit were very rude to them; they yelled at them, kicked or hit them and called them names because they were moving too slow. This grieved my spirit because I knew their attitude was wrong and non-Christian. We were in their country and in their town. They were nice to move from their homes to allow bombing and for us to practice our shooting.

As I continued to work at the correctional center, I was always on the lookout for the different changes that occurred often. Every day was different, and I was always on my guard. I enjoyed having a job that helped me to take care of my family, especially when my wife was laid off work. My first thanks went to God for this job that was a very nice-paying job. As a family, we were able to take vacations and have provisions too.

Some of the places we visit were usually in the state. We wanted the children to get a better view of Illinois. We went to a place called Hole in the Rock. It was about sixty miles from Centralia. I often got information about the sites we visited from other people who had been there. I was always interested in places that were children-friendly and interesting. Novella and I always thought about our children first; we would not leave them with babysitters because we loved having them around. Family has always been very important to us. We would, as a family, go to parks, movies, and just take rides throughout the state. The children would always remind us that we took them away from family, moving them to the north away from everything they knew as family, and this was our way to make up for our move from the South to the North. The children would remind us that we were seven hundred miles away from family.

On weekends, church was our first priority. After church, we would drive out to the rural area of Centralia. The countryside was full of fruit trees, and Novella and I loved to go and pick fruit along with the children.

I also believe that this was the connection for us with our home state of Louisiana. Louisiana is full of every kind of fruit tree you can imagine. As children, we could literally live off the fruit from trees and vines, most of which grew naturally in most areas. These drives allowed us to not be lonely and enjoy each other's company. It also gave us some wonderful memories. We loved spending time with our children, and we still do. We would like for all of us to get together in one big reunion, and I know God will allow that to happen.

The North offered more interaction between whites and blacks than the South did for me. The North allowed me to consider some whites as friends. This was not the case in the South. In the South, we stuck together as family, and that circle was wrapped pretty tight; but in the North, I had real friends who happened to be white. I remember one man I worked with who lived on a farm. He invited Novella and me to visit his house often. He and his wife were really nice people, and we enjoyed their company. The only problem with my friend was that he was very tight with his money. He always seemed to think that he could do any needed carpentry work around his house. His wife disagreed because she felt that he was a cluck with his hands and that she would have to get someone to repair his work. They were pretty amusing to be around, and we enjoyed their stories. I remember one story where she got a tractor and plowed over a room extension he had added to the house. The both of them were a lot of fun. He said, "She was a mess." And she said that "his work was a mess."

CHAPTER EIGHTEEN

My Children

I always thanked God for my children because they all have great personalities, and they all have kind hearts. I determined this by their actions in certain situations. They were all raised to love God, and Novella and I made sure they went to church and Sunday school. We decided, before we had children, that they would be raised in the church and that we would take them to church, not send them to church. The two things we made sure that our children knew before they attended school were their ABCs and the Lord's Prayer. I was thankful that my wife and I both had a strong Christian background to pull knowledge from. We came from good old Baptist Christian backgrounds. I believe any relationship should have a strong foundation, and there is no other foundation stronger than Jesus Christ our Lord. All else is sinking sand.

I always give thanks to my God for my children because when they were growing up, all of them had good character. First of all, we went to Sunday school and church with them every Sunday. We believed it is a parent's job to provide a religious education. When we were a young couple, we would go to church and see my wife's family in church. It was good for the children to see the family in church. That modeled to them that going to church was a tradition in our family, one that they would eventually pass on to their children.

When we came up north, we only had the three children: Reginald, Shari, and Rodney, but we had an addition to the family twelve years later. My wife became pregnant with our youngest son, Eric. Eric was a surprise for all of us, especially the children. They were all excited about their new sibling. It was so nice to see how they always made sure that their mom was comfortable. They always talked about the new baby and what their plan for the baby was. Before the baby was born, Reggie would come home on his lunch break from school to check on his mother. Shari was constantly teasing Rodney that he would not be the baby any longer, something she seemed to relish, although I did not know why. Rodney seemed to be happy not to be the baby anymore and excited to step into his role as a big brother after being the baby for so long. I thanked God for the blessing.

When Eric was born, we were all excited. The house was very busy. The children fought to take care of him. Shari treated him as though he were a baby doll, upset if anyone tried to take him away when she had him in her grip. When Eric was old enough to walk, they would take him to the park or any place that they wanted to go. He was the third wheel. I was amazed at how they loved him, and that was when I realized that all of them would be exceptional parents.

Reggie, who was on the basketball team, would even take him to basketball practice. The coach learned early on not to say too much against Eric coming to the practices after an incident that happened during practice one day. Eric loved to run and get the ball when it would travel out of bounds, and then run with it until one of the players caught up with him and retrieved it. This went on through the practices. Eric loved to throw balls. Well, one day, the coach told Reggie that Eric would have to leave practice; perhaps, on this day, Eric's behavior annoyed him.

Reggie said, "All right, coach." Then he started to pack up Eric's stuff and his.

The coach asked, "Where are you going?"

Reggie replied, "I'm leaving. If my brother cannot stay, then I'm leaving too."

The coach then told him to just keep Eric from the ball. I'm sure all the players helped to keep Eric away from the ball because they all got a kick out of him being there. He was so likable in that way. So all the older children's friends learned to put up with Eric always being around. The children all pitched in to help with Eric—even if we wanted to take him with us, they insisted that they would watch him. They all liked spending time with their baby brother.

I remember one day when Shari was watching him while Novella and I went to run an errand. When we returned, Shari was on the phone located in the kitchen. We walked in the kitchen and there was Eric on the floor, underneath her chair, next to the cabinets. We looked at Eric then back at Shari, who was talking profusely in a teen conversation. We asked her where Eric was, and she pointed to the floor realizing that we could see Eric, so she wondered why we would ask where he was. She continued to talk, and Novella and I, at this time, had stopped and were staring at her. She finally noticed us and our peculiar behavior, so she looked down on the floor and gasped. Eric had taken items out of the cabinets, and they were now scattered all over the floor. He seemed to be looking for a particular item. The item he was looking for was grease to spread on his hair; I guess he felt he needed some oil on his scalp. Eric's entire head was covered with Crisco oil. Shari hung up the phone and gave him a nice bath and shampoo, but his hair was oily for about a day or so.

It was so much fun watching the children with Eric. I loved the patience they all had with him. It assured me that they would some day be good parents, and they are. Eric was the epitome of a typical boy. Shari would say "he is so bad," but she would get mad if anyone spanked him.

I remember one time when Eric was about five years old, we bought him a tricycle. He loved riding the bike in and out of the house. We had a basement in our home, and the stairs to the basement was narrow and steep. I guess Eric had seen a TV show where people rode bikes down the stairs. All of a sudden, we heard bump after bump in the back where the basement was located. There was Eric riding that tricycle down the stairs. We all were so thankful that he did not break any body parts, but we made sure to keep the bike in the garage after that stunt. He also was called Evel Knievel for a while. The scariest thing he did was when he went missing for thirty minutes. Everyone in the neighborhood looked for him; all the neighbors knew him and grew to love him too. If Eric would cry, doors seemed to open and inquiries were made as to why he was crying. Well, the day he went missing, we all searched and searched for him. Finally, we decided to call the police. The phone rang, and the woman on the other end asked if we had anyone missing. We said yes, our son. She laughed and acknowledged who she was, and I let out a sigh of relief. The lady on the other end of the phone was our neighborhood grocer. We knew both she and her husband very well because we shopped at her store often. She laughed and said that Eric was at the store trying to purchase some candy and a small cake, and wanted it charged to his dad's bill. I was relieved and puzzled because the store was a block away from the house.

"How did he get there?" I asked.

"He rode his tricycle" was the response.

We both laughed, and she wanted to know what she should do. I told her to let him have the candy and cakes but to tell him to stay there until we got to the store. When we got to him, my wife asked him why he left the house and rode his bike to the store. He replied that he wanted some candy. He was fine, but he continued to get into things that would keep the entire family on our toes.

CHAPTER NINETEEN

My Son's Dog, Deo

Deo was Eric's first pet, he even named him. He was a black bird-dog with long ears. Eric would spend hours playing with him. Deo had a doghouse in the back yard that Eric would go inside of to play with the dog. The one thing that his mother did not like was Eric going inside of the doghouse. Another thing she did not like was that every time she tried to punish Eric for something he did, he would run to the doghouse and get behind Deo who would protect him. When my wife tried to reach for him, the dog would growl at her. My wife would scream for Eric to come out, but he would stay safely behind the dog. Hours later, he would come out thinking that Novella had forgotten about the punishment, but she would always remember and put him in time-out. We loved that dog, but no one loved him more than Eric. The neighbors liked the dog too. One day, when Novella was trying to get to Eric, who had ran and hid behind Deo again, she heard someone say, "Shame, shame, shame. How can you be so mean as to yell at a dog and a little boy?"

When the children started going off to college, we saw a big difference in the house. Eric missed them a lot; we could tell by his behavior. He was always asking when they would be coming home or when we would be going to visit them. I remember one time, we were at Shari's campus signing her up for her first apartment. Novella and I were in the office with the manager, and Reggie was outside with Eric by the pool the complex owned. All of a sudden, a girl came into the office and said that she just witnessed the most amazing thing. She said that a little boy just jumped in the pool outside with all his clothes on. Novella and I moved at the same time. We knew who the little kid was that jumped in the pool. Reggie had to fish him out, but he was soaked from his head to his feet. When Eric got out of the water, he said, "Reggie, I hold my breath."

The college trips were fun for Novella and me. We enjoyed visiting the different campuses and meeting our children's friends. They came from all over the world, and it was interesting talking to them. When Eric grew up, he attended college too. In high school, he wrestled and played baseball. He went on to play minor league ball for the Kansas City Royals. He played for three years, and his batting average was 319—that was really over-average for a young player. He wanted to go to the major leagues, but after three years in the minor, he decided to go back to school and finish his education. He met and married a nice girl, and they live in St. Louis, Missouri. He has two children, and the children are such a joy to watch. I can see Eric in his children, so smart, so intense. I'm praying that his son makes the major leagues because he certainly has the talent. His daughter is nothing to sneeze at either; she looks as if she will be able to play sports. She is tall and focused.

I am thankful to God for all my children and their families. They all went to college, and they all have great careers. I love my children, and I am so proud of all of them. I am proud of all their accomplishments and their determination. I'm proud of their parenting skills and their attitudes toward life, but the one thing I'm most proud of is their relationship with Jesus Christ and God.

All my children went to college and have careers, which afforded them a comfortable lifestyle. My oldest son has his own business in real estate. He and his wife have four children and two foster children that they raised. My daughter is a high school teacher. She and her husband have four children. My second son had an outstanding career in corrections. He went all the way to warden; he was able to retire before all his siblings. He and his wife have two children. My baby son and his wife have two children.

I know that God has been with me. God has brought us safely this far, and I do believe that grace will lead us on. I've always taught my children that in America, you can be who you want to be. From my experiences in other countries, I know this to be true. I encouraged them to go for it, and if at first they did not succeed, to try again. You might fall down, but get back up and try again. Success is not promised to the swift, strong, or bold, but it is given to the one who keeps going to the end. The payment or success of all situations will end with the teachings of Jesus Christ, living with him in eternity.

CHAPTER TWENTY

Retirement

I started out in corrections as an officer in Vandalia, Illinois. I worked at Vandalia Correctional Center for over ten years. I was very excited when the state decided to build a correctional center in the town I lived in. The distance from Vandalia to Centralia was thirty miles, so I was going to save energy and time by transferring to the newly built center in Centralia. The center was of the same level as the one in Vandalia. The number of inmates was 750; the dial on the center was medium security just like in Vandalia. I was assigned to the prison, and I found myself having a lot of free time. I did not realize that driving sixty miles a day could exhaust so much time. I enjoyed the freedom of not having to drive so much and used my extra time to read books. I loved reading but had not found the time to read for enjoyment in quite a while. I started reading the Bible more. I invested in a one-year Bible, and I would recommend it to everyone. The Bible is outlined and dated for you so you know exactly where you are suppose to be and the date you are on. I read from January to December and completed the entire Bible. I had not read the entire Bible before and was so thankful that I was able to read it from start to finish. But if you attend Sunday school, you will have covered the Bible from start to finish in seven years. The Sunday school material is designed for the coverage of the entire Bible in a seven-year time frame. So with that in mind, I have probably read the entire Bible quite a few times because my family and I attended Sunday school and church regularly.

My new assignment at Centralia Correctional Center was a relief from driving. My duties were slightly different too. I was assigned to work in the towers at the facility. It was an all right assignment but got a little lonely. I was away from staff and inmates; my duties were to sit in a tower and keep watch over the correctional facility. I used to listen to my radio at a low volume, something to keep me occupied. I did not want to take my eyes off the grounds, so I really did not want to get engrossed in a book. I did not understand why they did not want me to listen to the radio at all, but I abided by their rules. This rule to me was not acceptable because I needed to be mentally alert just in case something happened. It was next to impossible to sit in one spot for eight hours and not get bored—and boredom leads to drowsiness. I felt like the facility was new and had these new ideas that just were not acceptable. So for the first time in my career, I decided to not abide by this particular rule. The radio kept me alert; therefore, the people who depended on me to be alert would not be disappointed. I found a way to have my radio in the tower; I placed my radio in a hole that was in the wall with only the wire being visible. It had two connecting wires, but only a little wire could be seen. So when the officer came around to check, he would only see a little hole in the wall and think nothing of it. Remember, this is corrections; we have so much more to be concerned about than a little hole in the wall. So they never found the radio in the tower, and I said my prayers. This made the day seem to move faster. I thank God for giving me such a comfortable way to make a living and to help my fellowmen at the same time.

The facility was closer to home, but the location of the facility was sometimes hard to get to when it rained. This only happened to me once, but it took me an extra thirty minutes to get to work. The area that the center was in was set low in the city, and when it rained hard, the streets would flood, and the cars could not move safely down the road. The rain would cover the road so the cars had to turn around and go a different way. This was about twenty minutes out of the way, but this only happened one time in the years that I worked there.

I had been in Centralia for fifteen years, and my older children were in college. My baby son was at home with Novella and me. He was getting lonely because now the house was not full of people. Novella and I decided to adopt a little girl. We always wanted a second daughter but were never able to have one. Shari was our only daughter, and she was enough to quench our desire for one. She is such a good daughter, and I thank God for her daily.

We took our time, and God sent us a beautiful little one-year-old whom we named Crystal Bernice. She and Eric got along well, and we had the joy of watching the two of them get into all kinds of mischievousness. I recall one time that my wife and I took off for the weekend. We decided to visit Kansa City, which was a 150-mile trip. Well, when we got to the hotel, Novella only had one check left in her checkbook. So we decided to write the check over the amount it would cost to stay at the hotel and use the money for our other needs. Novella and I were drained mentally and physically wondering how we could have overlooked the checkbook folly. So we got to the room and turned on the air-conditioner. Soon there was a knock at our door. It was hotel security standing there with Crystal and Eric. He asked if they were ours. I started to say no, but God would not have liked that. I retrieved the two not without the security guard telling me, with a disapproving look on his face, that they were in the bar section. How they got there? I have no idea, but those two were a handful. We often traveled with the children because it was very relaxing to all of us. The kids would often sing songs in the backseat of the car before dozing off to sleep. We enjoyed going to ball games, fishing, and we loved family picnics. Eric and Crystal were so much fun, but the real fun started with the grandchildren.

I remember once, we took Shari's children with us on one of our fishing trips. Shari's oldest daughter, India, was fishing alongside of us. Novella pulled her line out of the water with a big fish hooked to it. The fish hit India on her thigh, and she said, "Grandmother, you hit me with your fish." Novella told her how sorry she was that the fish hit her. India held her little leg for about an hour. Joshua was always the tough one looking out for his sisters. I remember on one of their visits, the younger daughter, Gariel, got into an anthill. Her little legs had red ants all over them. Joshua and India tried to rub them off, and eventually, they brought her inside to us. After we applied medicine to her legs, Joshua went outside for revenge. He stomped the anthill into a flattened surface of dirt. He was very upset with them for biting his baby sister.

I remember one time when Reggie's children were visiting, we again loaded the grandchildren into the car as we used to do with their parents and headed to the nearest fishing hole. The fish were biting, and we were happy to have our grandchildren with us. Reggie's daughter wanted Novella to put the worm on her hook. So Novella put the worm on her own hook, and then she went to where Corsica was to put the worm on her hook. While Novella was hooking Corsica's pole, Corsica started to laugh. She said, "Grandma, look! Your pole is swimming away." Corsica thought that was the funniest thing ever. About ten minutes later, the pole floated back to where we were, and I was able to reach in the water and retrieve it. There was a big fish attached to the hook, which was a nice surprise for us all.

Novella and I always stayed busy. We would travel to Louisiana and visit friends whom we had not seen for a long time. I would write songs, and one of my songs was published. I never submitted any more, but it was something to keep me occupied. My daughter tells me that her children like to write music. I know they get that from my genes. Novella was working for the state of Illinois too, and she got to know a lot of people. She was even present when the governor signed bills for the state. We always followed God's lead, and that kept us full of life.

After being in Centralia and working at their facility for five years, I was ready for a change. Correctional facilities were popping up all over the state, so I decided to transfer to a new one in a place called Oneida, Illinois. This was the place I retired from as a sergeant. This meant more money and more responsibility. My middle son joined me in the corrections field, and I was glad that he did.

At this time, my wife had a foster home, and this kept us very busy. The house was back to being filled with adventure and excitement. My wife still worked for family services too. We were busy, but I found myself wanting to retire. I enjoyed my new position as a sergeant but found it to be problematic with the staff. I was in charge of four units a day. My duties included making sure the units were safe and the staff was abiding by the rules and regulations. There seemed to always be someone not happy about something. I enjoyed being in a state of peace, and you cannot remain in that state as a supervisor in the department of corrections. One day, a man was going around talking to certain people about retiring early. I talked with the man, and he gave me the retiring age criteria. I'm thankful that retiring early was an option. I filled out the paperwork and set the date of my retirement. I decided to finish the year and retire at the end of the year.

CHAPTER TWENTY-ONE

Building the Church

Retiring early afforded me the time to look around and search for a place to retire too. We looked in different cities and states and found that it was nice to be able to have choices. This also gave us free time to do more work at the church. The congregation was discussing building a new church building. The Macedonia Baptist Church building was getting very old and worn out. There were a lot of repairs needed, actually too many to try and repair. To make things even more complicated, a huge storm swept through our town. The storm brought high winds that damaged a lot of homes in the area. Macedonia was hit hard; the building all but collapsed from the rage of the storm. The physical loss was very hard for the members of the church, but as hard as the physical loss seemed to be, nothing hit us harder than losing our beloved pastor. The congregation found itself without a church building and without our pastor. With our leader gone and the building close to destruction, our members wanted to give up. I was the only deacon at the church, so the leadership role was thrust on me. With all seeming lost, the members asked, "What are we going to do now?" My response was "we are going to have church."

The church was insured for 120 thousand dollars. The insurance company, at first, refused to pay on our claim. The congregation formed committees to work as spokesmen for the church, but the insurance company still refused to pay. So we had to get a lawyer, and the lawyer got the insurance company to pay the claim. We were all so happy. We still were having church in a trailer we rented until the new church was built. We worked together on the new church, and the finished building is beautiful. If you ever go through Centralia, Illinois, stop by and visit Macedonia Baptist church.

After the church was finished, Novella and I decided that our job was done in Illinois. We had completed our journey in Centralia. It had been thirty years. God allowed us to be blessed and to be a blessing. God knows all and sees all. I believe we were sent there to build the church after the storm knocked it down. We had a big celebration and an open house for the community to see how God had blessed the church, and it was very nice. Everything seemed to work together for the good. The retiring, the church, and now after searching for a place to retire, we found a place. The town is a small town in Louisiana named Kentwood. I even found a part-time job there as a deputy sheriff.

Thinking of a title for the book, I decided on 30 South/30 North. The first 30 represents my years as a Southerner, and the second 30 represents my life living up north. As a matter of fact, the number 30 has always had a significant place in my life. The code that our family used in case of an emergency was "that will be thirty for the day." We taught our children that if we ever called or if they were ever in trouble, that was the code to use to let one another know to come quickly. Even with my wife's foster children, she taught them the code. If any of them were ever in danger and someone was around where they could not speak openly about an emergency, she trained them to say "that's thirty for today" so she would know that they were in some sort of trouble.

I love to be asked which place I liked living in best. I am frequently asked "do you like the North or South better?" My response is that the South has hot weather, and the North has cold weather. The people, to me, are like the weather. The people in the South are warmer, friendlier, and the people in the North are cooler with forming friendships. But the money in the North is better; the salary in the North is better than in the South. When I had to earn a salary, the North was my choice to live, but when I wanted to relax, I would prefer the South.

My youngest son, who was born in the north, comes to visit me often. He would always say that the only thing wrong with the South is that it is too far from the North.

I thank God daily for my family and the great blessings God has given us. I just would like to share with the world these words. *Life is what you make out of it.* There has been a lot of discussion concerning world problems and concerns. I have the answer, and the answer is Jesus Christ. Jesus is the answer to the young and the old, the rich and the poor. Everyone should read the Bible and learn about him. May God bless all who see and read this book.